THE COMPLETE WEBER WOOD PELLET GRILL COOKBOOK

1000-DAY IRRESISTIBLE MEAT, FISH, VEGETABLE RECIPES FOR YOUR WOOD PELLET GRILL

GAIL MCKELVY

Copyright © 2021 by Gail McKelvy- All rights reserved.

The content contained within this book may not be reproduced, duplicated, or transmitted without direct written permission from the author or the publisher. Under no circumstances will any blame or legal responsibility be held against the publisher, or author, for any damages, reparation, or monetary loss due to the information contained within this book, either directly or indirectly.

Legal Notice: This book is copyright protected. It is only for personal use. You cannot amend, distribute, sell, use, quote or paraphrase any part, or the content within this book, without the consent of the author or publisher.

Disclaimer Notice: Please note the information contained within this document is for educational and entertainment purposes only. All effort has been executed to present accurate, up to date, reliable, complete information. No warranties of any kind are declared or implied. Readers acknowledge that the author is not engaged in the rendering of legal, financial, medical, or professional advice. The content within this book has been derived from various sources. Please consult a licensed professional before attempting any techniques outlined in this book. By reading this document, the reader agrees that under no circumstances is the author responsible for any losses, direct or indirect, that are incurred as a result of the use of the information contained within this document, including, but not limited to, errors, omissions, or inaccuracies.

CONTENTS

INTRODUCTION 7
    What Wood Pellet Grills Are 7
    How the Weber Wood Pellet Grill Works 7
    The Benefits You'll Gain from Your Weber Wood Pellet Grill 7
    Using Tips for Your Weber Wood Pellet Grill 8
    Better to Clean Your Weber Wood Pellet Grill 9

SEAFOOD RECIPES 11
    Smoked Salt Cured Lox 11
    Cured Cold-smoked Lox 12
    Bacon Wrapped Scallops 13
    Oysters In The Shell 14
    Grilled Tilapia With Blistered Cherry Tomatoes 15
    Simple Glazed Salmon Fillets 16
    Cedar Smoked Garlic Salmon 17
    Garlic Pepper Shrimp Pesto Bruschetta 18
    Spicy Lime Shrimp 19
    Traeger Jerk Shrimp 20
    Grilled Lobster Tails With Smoked Paprika Butter 21
    Grilled Shrimp Brochette 22
    Lobster Tail 23
    Smoked Trout 24

BAKING RECIPES 25
    Spiced Carrot Cake 25
    Chocolate Peanut Cookies 26
    Sourdough Pizza 27
    Savory Cheesecake With Bourbon Pecan Topping 28
    Baked Cast Iron Berry Cobbler 29
    Grilled Beer Cheese Dip 30
    Sweet Cheese Muffins 31
    Garlic Cheese Pull Apart Bread 32

Baked Buttermilk Biscuits 33
The Dan Patrick Show Pull-apart Pesto Bread 34
Baked Wood-fired Pizza 35
Basil Margherita Pizza 36
Cornbread Chicken Stuffing 37
Chocolate Lava Cake With Smoked Whipped Cream 38

PORK RECIPES 39
Smoky Pork Tenderloin 39
Smoked Bbq Ribs 40
Smoked Porchetta With Italian Salsa Verde 41
Smoked Traeger Pulled Pork 42
Double Smoked Apple Spiral Ham 43
Bbq Pulled Pork Grilled Cheese Sandwich 44
Traeger Smoked Sausage 45
Pork Tenderloin 46
Pig On A Stick With Buffalo Glaze 47
Egg Bacon French Toast Panini 48
Bacon Grilled Cheese Sandwich 49
Bbq Pulled Coleslaw Pork Sandwiches 50
Smoked Ribs 51
Roasted Pork With Balsamic Strawberry Sauce 52

POULTRY RECIPES 53
Oktoberfest Pretzel Mustard Chicken 53
Cheese Chicken Cordon Bleu 54
Grilled Beantown Chicken Wings 55
Grilled Parmesan Chicken Wings 56
Bbq Chicken Tostada 57
Green Goddess Chicken Legs 58
Savory Jerk Chicken Wings 59
Cheese Buffalo Chicken Wings 60
Applewood-smoked Whole Turkey 61
Cajun Brined Maple Smoked Turkey Breast 62

Cornish Game Hens 63
Spatchcocked Turkey 64
Cider-brined Turkey 65
Chicken Egg Rolls With Buffalo Sauce 66

VEGETABLES RECIPES 67

Roasted Pumpkin Seeds 67
Tater Tot Bake 68
Smoked Pickled Green Beans 69
Roasted Olives 70
Roasted Jalapeno Cheddar Deviled Eggs 71
Traeger Smoked Coleslaw 72
Baked Sweet Potato Casserole With Marshmallow Fluff 73
Grilled Corn On The Cob With Parmesan And Garlic 74
Red Potato Grilled Lollipops 75
Grilled Ratatouille Salad 76
Smoked Jalapeño Poppers 77
Roasted Do-ahead Mashed Potatoes 78
Roasted New Potatoes With Compound Butter 79
Sicilian Stuffed Mushrooms 80

BEEF LAMB AND GAME RECIPES 81

Bbq Elk Shoulder 81
Korean Style Bbq Prime Ribs 82
Rosemary Prime Rib 83
Bbq Bacon Meatballs 84
Smoked Pot Roast Brisket 85
Smoked New York Steaks 86
Roasted Mustard Crusted Prime Rib 87
Pan Seared Parsley Ribeye Steak 88
Savory Smoked Beef Short Ribs 89
Steak Tips With Mashed Potatoes 90
Texas Seared Beef 91
Grilled Garlic Tomahawk Steak 92

Savory Cheese Steak Rolls With Puff Pastry 93
Grilled Lemon Skirt Steak 94

APPETIZERS AND SNACKS 95
Pigs In A Blanket 95
Chicken Wings With Teriyaki Glaze 96
Bayou Wings With Cajun Rémoulade 97
Cold-smoked Cheese 98
Chorizo Queso Fundido 99
Delicious Deviled Crab Appetizer 100
Citrus-infused Marinated Olives 101
Pulled Pork Loaded Nachos 102
Deviled Eggs With Smoked Paprika 103
Pig Pops (sweet-hot Bacon On A Stick) 104
Jalapeño Poppers With Chipotle Sour Cream 105
Grilled Guacamole 106
Sriracha & Maple Cashews 107
Bacon-wrapped Jalapeño Poppers 108

COCKTAILS RECIPES 109
Smoked Mulled Wine 109
Bacon Old-fashioned Cocktail 110
Traeger Old Fashioned 111
Smoked Apple Cider 112
Grilled Peach Sour Cocktail 113
Traeger Gin & Tonic 114
Smoked Eggnog 115
Smoked Berry Cocktail 116
In Traeger Fashion Cocktail 117
Smoked Raspberry Bubbler Cocktail 118
Smoked Hibiscus Sparkler 119
Cran-apple Tequila Punch With Smoked Oranges 120

INTRODUCTION

What Wood Pellet Grills Are

A wood pellet grill is basically a hybrid between a smoker, a traditional grill, and an oven. They can be used for many different types of cooking, even searing and baking. Wood pellets are used for fuel. Some wood pellets are meant to last a long time, while others focus on enhancing flavor.

Pellet grills do not cook food over a direct flame. Instead, they heat food indirectly by circulating the warmth through the grill, much like what an oven does.

How the Weber Wood Pellet Grill Works

A pellet grill looks like a gas grill, with a metal hopper mounted to one side to house the wood pellets they burn as fuel. The resulting fire imparts a smoky taste because the wood pellets are made from flavorful hardwood species such as hickory, oak, pecan, and cherry.

Today's pellet grills feature an electronic thermostat with a digital display, so you can dial in a precise cooking temperature; the hopper automatically draws the appropriate amount of pellets into the firebox, where they're ignited. The grill holds the temperature steady, like an oven, adjusting the rate at which it burns pellets to maintain that set temperature.

The Benefits You'll Gain from Your Weber Wood Pellet Grill

There are some key advantages to be enjoyed when using a pellet smoker. We've covered the most important below.

1. A pellet smoker offers more options and versatility than a standard smoker. Depending on the model you choose, it will be possible to roast, smoke, barbecue, and even bake inside your pellet smoker.
2. Pellet smoking offers the best results for smoked meat. This is because they are designed specifically to infuse maximum smoke flavor with indirect heat. When compared to smoking in a normal grill, the results are far better. For rich and complex flavor, a dedicated pellet smoker is an ideal choice.
3. Flavor options are virtually unlimited. Pellet chips are made from natural wood pieces, with flavors like hickory, maple, apple, mesquite, cherry, and more.

4. Temperature management is simple because most pellet smokers have advanced designs with automatic timing and heat control. The hopper ensures a consistent level of smoke throughout cooking.
5. Most models reach smoking temperature within ten to fifteen minutes. Only gas grills are easier and faster to get to cooking temperature.
6. Pellet smokers are designed for serious home cooks, so they are generally large, offering plenty of cooking space. This means you can easily cook whole turkeys, chicken, duck and other game, large BBQ cuts, and anything else that you want to infuse with a rich flavor.
7. Unlike a charcoal or gas smoker, pellet models are easy to use. There's no need to measure or weigh the wood that you will use. Pellets are distributed as needed and cooking temperature is regulated by an electronic thermostat.
8. Value is incredible because a high-quality pellet smoker will last for many years without problems. Even though the initial price might be higher than a comparable gas or charcoal grill, longevity, ease of use, and amazing results add value.

Using Tips for Your Weber Wood Pellet Grill

1. Take advantage of your pellet grill's searing capabilities.

Many pellet grills feature searing capabilities, meaning they can reach temperatures over 500 degrees. Again, check your owner's manual for information on your specific model.

2. Use lower temperatures to generate more smoke.

You'll generate more smoke at lower temperatures, particularly in the "low and slow" range between 225 and 275.

3. Use the reverse sear method.

Don't be afraid to smoke your meat at a lower temperature, then finish it at a higher temperature. This two-step approach is especially useful for smoking chicken with crisp (not rubbery) skin, or the "reverse sear method" often employed for thicker steaks or prime rib

4. Never allow the pellets in the pellet hopper to run out.

Never allow the pellets in the pellet hopper to run out. If this happens, consult your owner's manual before relighting the grill. If you must, set a timer to remind yourself to top off the pellets.

5. Experiment with pellet flavors.

Experiment with pellet flavors. Some brands of pellets are fairly subtle.

Better to Clean Your Weber Wood Pellet Grill

It is often easiest to clean the inside of your grill at the same time as the outside because your grill will already be unplugged, cold and emptied of wood pellets. Cleaning the inside of your pellet smoker involves several steps to ensure proper pellet grill maintenance, including cleaning the grease drip tray, vacuuming and scraping the burn pot and scrubbing the grill grates.

1. GREASE DRIP TRAY

To clean the grease drip tray, first remove the grill grates and any extra cooking racks. Use a griddle scraper to scrub grease off of the surface of the tray and remove the scrubbed grease using a paper towel. Wipe the grease drip tray clean using a cloth or paper towel. If you want to clean your grease drip tray with soapy water or liquid cleaner, remove the tray from the BBQ first. Dry the tray completely before putting it back into your pellet smoker.

2. BURN POT

Regular pellet grill ash clean-out keeps your smoker operating in top condition. A clean smoker provides even cooking and produce the best tasting pulled pork, ribs, and grilled veggies — or anything else you want to cook.

To clean your burn pot, first remove the grease drip tray and heat deflector to access the burn pot. Pay attention to how they are installed so you can put them back in when you are done. The burn pot will often have a lot of ash build-up and debris that you will need to remove. The simplest way to clean your pellet smoker's burn pot is with a vacuum cleaner or ash vac. Use the hose to suck out all the ash and then wipe away any remaining ash or soot using a clean rag.

When deep cleaning your pellet grill after winter, you can take this a few steps further and scrub the interior walls of the smoker to remove any accumulated grease or dirt. After vacuuming the ash, use a scraper with a flat edge to dislodge scale from the sides of the smoker chamber. Scrub the loosened dirt with a non-metallic brush and wipe the fire pot with a clean cloth.

You can use a damp cloth to wipe the interior of the grill, but never put water directly into the burn pot. Use caution not to damage the electric elements and allow the grill to dry completely before use. Once your burn pot is clean, replace the heat deflector, drip tray, and grates.

If your grill is equipped with an ash container, now is a great time to empty it. Ash collection systems make it easy to remove ash build-up and allow you to clean your burn pot less often, as they collect much of the ash that normally builds up inside your pellet smoker.

3. GRILL GRATES

Cleaning your pellet smoker grates every time you use your grill keeps your food tasting delicious and fresh so your cookout guests are always satisfied. There are two ways to clean your grill grates; cold or hot. Follow these steps for how to clean your grill before or after use:

Cold Method (Before Cooking):

Ensure your grill is unplugged and cool:

Remove grates from grill and clean with bbq degreaser or soap and water. Some pellet grills may have dishwasher safe grates. If not, they can be cleaned in a sink or with a pressure washer or garden hose. If they are painted, be careful with using a pressure washer.

Scrub the grates thoroughly: Use a brush or spatula to scrub the grates to remove any residue that remains.

Hot Method (After Cooking):

Set your grill to the highest temperature: Grill grates are easiest to clean when they are hot — and your grill will do most of the work for you. After you cook, turn your grill to the highest temperature and allow it to heat up completely.

Do a burn off: Wait 10 to 15 minutes to let your grill burn away the remaining food and grease on the grill grates. Performing a burn off loosens any stuck-on grease and makes it easy to scrape off the ash.

Scrub the grates thoroughly: Use a brush or spatula to scrub the grates to remove any residue that remains. Because the grill will be hot, it is best to use a long-handled brush or scraper. You may also choose to clean your grill grates while wearing an oven mitt or grill glove to prevent burns.

SEAFOOD RECIPES

Smoked Salt Cured Lox

Servings: 8

Cooking Time: 30 Minutes

Ingredients:
- 1 Cup kosher salt
- 1 Cup sugar
- 1 Tablespoon cracked black pepper
- 1 Whole lemon zest
- 1 Whole orange zest
- 1 Whole Packaged Dill, roughly chopped including stems
- 2 Pound salmon fillet, skin on

Directions:
1. Mix together salt, sugar, black pepper, lemon zest, orange zest, and dill.
2. Slice salmon in half. Coat all flesh of salmon completely with salt sugar mixture. Sandwich the 2 pieces together, flesh to flesh and completely cover with salt sugar mixture.
3. Wrap tightly with plastic wrap and place into a gallon zip top bag. Squeeze out as much air as possible. Place wrapped salmon into a baking dish and place something heavy on top like a pot filled with water or a brick wrapped in foil. Place into the refrigerator for 10 hours. After 10 hours, flip over and put the weight back on top. Refrigerate for another 10 hours.
4. Remove from refrigerator, unwrap and rinse of remaining salt with cold water. Pat dry and leave on counter for 1 hour.
5. Supply your smoker with wood pellets and follow the start-up procedure. Preheat the grill, with the lid closed, to 180° F.
6. Place salmon onto a baking pan. Fill another baking pan with ice and place baking pan with salmon over ice.
7. Place onto grill and smoke for 30 minutes. Remove from grill and slice thin. Grill: 180 °F
8. Serve with bagels, cream cheese, capers, dill, lemon wedges, sliced tomatoes, and red onion. Enjoy!

Cured Cold-smoked Lox

Servings: 6   Cooking Time: 360 Minutes

Ingredients:
- ¼ cup salt
- ¼ cup sugar
- 1 tablespoon freshly ground black pepper
- 1 bunch dill, chopped
- 1 pound sashimi-grade salmon, skin removed
- 1 avocado, sliced
- 8 bagels
- 4 ounces cream cheese
- 1 bunch alfalfa sprouts
- 1 (3.5-ounce) jar capers

Directions:
1. In a small bowl, combine the salt, sugar, pepper, and fresh dill to make the curing mixture. Set aside.
2. On a smooth surface, lay out a large piece of plastic wrap and spread half of the curing salt mixture in the middle, spreading it out to about the size of the salmon.
3. Place the salmon on top of the curing salt.
4. Top the fish with the remaining curing salt, covering it completely. Wrap the salmon, leaving the ends open to drain.
5. Place the wrapped fish in a rimmed baking pan or dish lined with paper towels to soak up liquid.
6. Place a weight on the salmon evenly, such as a pan with a couple of heavy jars of pickles on top.
7. Put the salmon pan with weights in the refrigerator. Place something (a dishtowel, for example) under the back of the pan in order to slightly tip it down so the liquid drains away from the fish.
8. Leave the salmon to cure in the refrigerator for 24 hours.
9. Place the wood pellets in the smoker, but do not follow the start-up procedure and do not preheat.
10. Remove the salmon from the refrigerator, unwrap it, rinse it off, and pat dry.
11. Put the salmon in the smoker while still cold from the refrigerator to slow down the cooking process. You'll need to use a cold-smoker attachment or enlist the help of a smoker tube to hold the temperature at 80°F and maintain that for 6 hours to absorb smoke and complete the cold-smoking process.
12. Remove the salmon from the smoker, place it in a sealed plastic bag, and refrigerate for 24 hours. The salmon will be translucent all the way through.
13. Thinly slice the lox and serve with sliced avocado, bagels, cream cheese, alfalfa sprouts, and capers.

Bacon Wrapped Scallops

Servings: 8

Cooking Time: 20 Minutes

Ingredients:
- 24 jumbo deep sea diver scallops, dry-packed
- 1/2 Cup butter
- salt
- freshly ground black pepper
- 1 Clove garlic, minced
- 12 Slices thin-cut bacon, cut in half crosswise
- lemon wedges, for serving

Directions:
1. Remove the small, crescent-shaped muscle from the side of each scallop, if still attached. Dry the scallops thoroughly on paper towels, then transfer to a medium bowl.
2. Melt butter in a small saucepan, add garlic and cook for 1 minute. Let cool slightly then pour over the scallops. Season with salt and pepper and gently toss to coat.
3. Wrap a piece of bacon around each scallop and secure with a toothpick.
4. Supply your smoker with wood pellets and follow the start-up procedure. Preheat the grill, with the lid closed, to 400° F.
5. Arrange the scallops directly on the grill grate. Grill for 15 to 20 minutes, or until the scallop is opaque and the bacon has begun to crisp. If desired, you can turn the scallops on their side, bacon-side down, turning occasionally to crisp the bacon. Do not overcook. Grill: 400 °F
6. Transfer the scallops to a platter and serve with lemon wedges.

Oysters In The Shell

Servings: 4

Cooking Time: 20 Minutes

Ingredients:

- 8 medium oysters, unopened, in the shell, rinsed and scrubbed
- 1 batch Lemon Butter Mop for Seafood

Directions:

1. Supply your smoker with wood pellets and follow the start-up procedure. Preheat the grill, with the lid closed, to 375°F.

2. Place the unopened oysters directly on the grill grate and grill for about 20 minutes, or until the oysters are done and their shells open.

3. Discard any oysters that do not open. Shuck the remaining oysters, transfer them to a bowl, and add the mop. Serve immediately.

Grilled Tilapia With Blistered Cherry Tomatoes

Servings: 4   Cooking Time: 15 Minutes

Ingredients:

- 1½lb (680g) tilapia fillets or other mild white fish fillets
- chopped fresh curly or flat-leaf parsley
- for the marinade
- ½ cup extra virgin olive oil
- 1 garlic clove, peeled and smashed with a chef's knife
- 3 tbsp freshly squeezed lemon juice
- 1 tsp smoked paprika
- ½ tsp coarse salt
- ¼ tsp freshly ground black pepper
- for the tomatoes
- 2 tbsp extra virgin olive oil
- 2 pints (1 liter) cherry tomatoes (red, yellow, or heirloom varieties)
- coarse salt
- freshly ground black pepper

Directions:

1. Place a cast iron skillet on the grate. Supply your smoker with wood pellets and follow the start-up procedure. Preheat the grill, with the lid closed, to 400° F.
2. In a jar with a tight-fitting lid, make the marinade by combining the ingredients. Shake the jar vigorously to emulsify the ingredients.
3. Place the fillets in a single layer in a nonreactive baking dish. Pour half the marinade over them and turn the fillets to thoroughly coat. Cover with plastic wrap and refrigerate for 15 minutes. (Refrigerate no more than 30 minutes or the acid in the marinade will begin to cook the fish.)
4. Place the olive oil in the skillet. Add the tomatoes and season with salt and pepper. Stir to coat. Cook the tomatoes until they begin to blister and collapse, about 5 minutes, stirring once or twice. Remove the skillet from the grill and transfer the tomatoes to a bowl.
5. Carefully lift each fish fillet from the marinade and let the excess drip off. Place the fillets on the grate at a slight angle to the bars. Lightly season with salt and pepper. Grill until the fish flakes easily when pressed with a fork, about 4 to 5 minutes per side, turning carefully with a thin-bladed spatula.
6. Transfer the fillets to a warmed platter. Top with some of the tomatoes. (Place the remaining tomatoes in a serving bowl.) Scatter the parsley around the platter. Drizzle some of the remaining marinade over the top. Serve immediately.

Simple Glazed Salmon Fillets

Servings: 2

Cooking Time: 25 Minutes

Ingredients:

- 4 (6-8 oz) center-cut salmon fillets, skin on
- Fin & Feather Rub
- 1/2 Cup mayonnaise
- 2 Tablespoon Dijon mustard
- 1 Tablespoon fresh lemon juice
- 1 Tablespoon fresh chopped tarragon or dill
- lemon wedges

Directions:

1. Season the fillets with the Traeger Fin & Feather Rub.
2. Make the Glaze: Combine the mayonnaise and mustard in a small bowl. Stir in the lemon juice and dill or tarragon.
3. Spread the flesh-side of the fillets with the glaze.
4. Supply your smoker with wood pellets and follow the start-up procedure. Preheat the grill, with the lid closed, to 350° F.
5. Arrange the salmon fillets on the grill grate, skin-side down. Grill for 25 to 30 minutes, or until the salmon is opaque and flakes easily with a fork. Grill: 350 °F
6. Transfer to a platter or plates, garnish with sliced lemons and chopped dill and serve immediately. Enjoy!

Cedar Smoked Garlic Salmon

Servings: 6

Cooking Time: 60 Minutes

Ingredients:
- 1 Tsp Black Pepper
- 3 Cedar Plank, Untreated
- 1 Tsp Garlic, Minced
- 1/3 Cup Olive Oil
- 1 Tsp Onion, Salt
- 1 Tsp Parsley, Minced Fresh
- 1 1/2 Tbsp Rice Vinegar
- 2 Salmon, Fillets (Skin Removed)
- 1 Tsp Sesame Oil
- 1/3 Cup Soy Sauce

Directions:
1. Soak the cedar planks in warm water for an hour or more.
2. In a bowl, mix together the olive oil, rice vinegar, sesame oil, soy sauce, and minced garlic.
3. Add in the salmon and let it marinate for about 30 minutes.
4. Start your grill on smoke with the lid open until a fire is established in the burn pot (3-7 minutes).
5. Supply your smoker with wood pellets and follow the start-up procedure. Preheat the grill, with the lid closed, to 225° F.
6. Place the planks on the grate. Once the boards start to smoke and crackle a little, it's ready for the fish.
7. Remove the fish from the marinade, season it with the onion powder, parsley and black pepper, then discard the marinade.
8. Place the salmon on the planks and grill until it reaches 140°F internal temperature (start checking temp after the salmon has been on the grill for 30 minutes).
9. Remove from the grill, let it rest for 10 minutes, then serve.

Garlic Pepper Shrimp Pesto Bruschetta

Servings: 12

Cooking Time: 15 Minutes

Ingredients:

- 12 Slices Bread, Baguette
- 1/2 Tsp Chili Pepper Flakes
- 1/2 Tsp Garlic Powder
- 4 Cloves Garlic, Minced
- 2 Tbsp Olive Oil
- 1/2 Tsp Paprika, Smoked
- 1/4 Tsp Parsley, Leaves
- Pepper
- Pesto
- Salt
- 12 Shrimp, Jumbo

Directions:

1. Supply your smoker with wood pellets and follow the start-up procedure. Preheat the grill, with the lid closed, to 350° F. Place the baguette slices on a baking sheet lined with foil. Stir together the olive oil, and minced garlic, then brush both sides of the baguette slices with the mix. Place the pan inside the grill, and bake for about 10-15 minutes.

2. In a skillet, add a splash of olive oil, shrimp, chili powder, garlic powder, smoked paprika, salt pepper, and grill on medium-high heat for about 5 minutes (until the shrimp is pink). Be sure to stir often. Once pink, remove pan from heat. Once the baguettes are toasted, let them cool for 5 minutes, then spread a layer of pesto onto each one, then top with a shrimp, and serve.

Spicy Lime Shrimp

Servings: 4

Cooking Time: 10 Minutes

Ingredients:
- 2 Tsp Chili Paste
- 1/2 Tsp Cumin
- 2 Cloves Garlic, Minced
- 1 Large Lime, Juiced
- 1/4 Tsp Paprika, Powder
- 1/4 Tsp Red Flakes Pepper
- 1/2 Tsp Salt

Directions:

1. In a bowl, whisk together the lime juice, olive oil, garlic, chili powder, cumin, paprika, salt, pepper, and red pepper flakes.
2. Then pour it into a resealable bag, add the shrimp, toss the coat, let it marinate for 30 minutes.
3. Supply your smoker with wood pellets and follow the start-up procedure. Preheat the grill, with the lid closed, to 400° F.
4. Next place the shrimp on skewers, place on the grill, and grill each side for about two minutes until it's done. One finished, remove the shrimp from the grill and enjoy!

Traeger Jerk Shrimp

Servings: 8

Cooking Time: 10 Minutes

Ingredients:

- 1 Tablespoon brown sugar
- 1 Tablespoon smoked paprika
- 1 Teaspoon garlic powder
- 1/4 Teaspoon Thyme, ground
- 1/4 Teaspoon ground cayenne pepper
- 1 Teaspoon sea salt
- 1 lime zest
- 2 Pound shrimp in shell
- 3 Tablespoon olive oil

Directions:

1. Combine spices, salt, and lime zest in a small bowl and mix. Place shrimp into a large bowl, then drizzle in the olive oil, Add the spice mixture and toss to combine, making sure every shrimp is kissed with deliciousness.
2. Supply your smoker with wood pellets and follow the start-up procedure. Preheat the grill, with the lid closed, to 450° F.
3. Arrange the shrimp on the grill and cook for 2 – 3 minutes per side, until firm, opaque, and cooked through. Grill: 450 °F
4. Serve with lime wedges, fresh cilantro, mint, and Caribbean Hot Pepper Sauce. Enjoy!

Grilled Lobster Tails With Smoked Paprika Butter

Servings: 4

Cooking Time: 10-12 Minutes

Ingredients:
- 4 lobster tails, each about 8 to 10oz (225 to 285g), thawed if frozen
- 3 lemons, 1 quartered lengthwise, 2 halved through their equators
- for the butter
- 1¼ cup unsalted butter, at room temperature
- 2 garlic cloves, peeled and finely minced
- 3 tbsp chopped fresh parsley
- 2 tbsp chopped fresh chives
- 1 tbsp freshly squeezed lemon juice
- 2 tsp finely chopped lemon zest
- 2 tsp smoked paprika
- 1 tsp coarse salt

Directions:

1. Supply your smoker with wood pellets and follow the start-up procedure. Preheat the grill, with the lid closed, to 450° F.

2. In a medium bowl, make the paprika butter by combining the ingredients. Beat with a wooden spoon until well blended.

3. Use a sharp, heavy knife or sturdy kitchen shears to cut lengthwise through the top shell of each lobster tail in a straight line toward the tail fin. Gently loosen the meat from the bottom shell and sides. Lift the meat through the slit you just made so the meat sits on top of the shell. Slip a lemon quarter underneath the meat (between the meat and the bottom shell) to keep it elevated. Spread 1 tablespoon of paprika butter on top of each lobster. Melt the remaining butter and keep it warm.

4. Place the lobster tails flesh side up and lemon halves cut sides down on the grate. Grill the lobsters until the flesh is white and opaque and the internal temperature of the lobster meat reaches 135 to 140°F (57 to 60°C), about 10 to 12 minutes, basting at least once with some of the melted butter. (Don't overcook or the lobster will become unpleasantly rubbery.)

5. Transfer the lobsters and the lemon halves to a platter. Divide the remaining melted butter between 4 ramekins before serving.

Grilled Shrimp Brochette

Servings: 6

Cooking Time: 20 Minutes

Ingredients:

- 1 Pound extra-large shrimp, peeled and deveined
- 6 Whole fresh jalapeños
- 8 Ounce block Monterey Jack cheese
- 1 Pound bacon
- 2 Tablespoon Meat Church The Gospel All-Purpose Rub
- oil

Directions:

1. Fillet shrimp open slightly and set aside. Core the jalapeños and cut them into small slivers. Slice the cheese into similar-sized slivers as the peppers. Cut the bacon slices in half.
2. Place one slice of jalapeño and one slice of cheese inside each shrimp. Wrap stuffed shrimp in a half piece of bacon and secure with a toothpick.
3. After you have constructed all of the shrimp, season lightly with Meat Church The Gospel All-Purpose Rub.
4. Supply your smoker with wood pellets and follow the start-up procedure. Preheat the grill, with the lid closed, to 425° F.
5. Lightly oil the grill grate then place shrimp directly on the grate. Cook for about 20 minutes, turning at least once halfway through. Shrimp should turn pink and bacon will begin to crisp up. Grill: 425 °F
6. Remove from the grill and let rest for at least 10 minutes. Enjoy!

Lobster Tail

Servings: 2

Cooking Time: 25 Minutes

Ingredients:
- 2 lobster tails
- Salt
- Freshly ground black pepper
- 1 batch Lemon Butter Mop for Seafood

Directions:

1. Supply your smoker with wood pellets and follow the start-up procedure. Preheat the grill, with the lid closed, to 375°F.
2. Using kitchen shears, slit the top of the lobster shells, through the center, nearly to the tail. Once cut, expose as much meat as you can through the cut shell.
3. Season the lobster tails all over with salt and pepper.
4. Place the tails directly on the grill grate and grill until their internal temperature reaches 145°F. Remove the lobster from the grill and serve with the mop on the side for dipping.

Smoked Trout

Servings: 6

Cooking Time: 120 Minutes

Ingredients:

- 8 rainbow trout fillets
- 1 Gallon water
- 1/4 Cup salt
- 1/2 Cup brown sugar
- 1 Tablespoon black pepper
- 2 Tablespoon soy sauce

Directions:

1. Clean the fresh fish and butterfly them.
2. For the Brine: Combine one gallon water, brown sugar, soy sauce, salt and pepper and stir until salt and sugar are dissolved. Brine the trout in the refrigerator for 60 minutes.
3. Supply your smoker with wood pellets and follow the start-up procedure. Preheat the grill, with the lid closed, to 225° F.
4. Remove the fish from the brine and pat dry. Place fish directly on grill grate for 1-1/2 to 2 hours, depending on the thickness of the trout. Fish is done when it turns opaque and starts to flake. Serve hot or cold. Enjoy! Grill: 225 °F
5. Fish is done when it turns opaque and starts to flake. Serve hot or cold. Enjoy!

BAKING RECIPES

Spiced Carrot Cake

Servings: 10   Cooking Time: 35 Minutes

Ingredients:

- 1/2 Cup Apple Sauce, Unsweetened
- 2 Tsp Baking Powder
- 1 Tsp Baking Soda
- 1 1/2 Cups Brown Sugar
- 1/2 Cup Butter, Room Temp
- 3/4 Cup Canola Oil
- 3 Cups Carrot, Grated
- 1 1/2 Tsp Cinnamon, Ground
- 2 (8-Ounce) Packages Cream Cheese, Room Temperature
- 4 Egg
- 2 Cups Flour, All-Purpose
- 1/2 Tsp Ginger, Ground
- 1/4 Tsp Nutmeg, Ground
- 1/2 Tsp Salt
- 1/2 Cup Sugar
- 3 Cups Sugar, Icing

Directions:

1. Supply your smoker with wood pellets and follow the start-up procedure. Preheat the grill, with the lid closed, to 350° F.
2. Line the bottom of 2 9-inch cake pans with parchment paper and spray the sides with cooking spray. Set aside.
3. In a large bowl, combine flour, baking powder and soda, spices and salt.
4. In a smaller bowl, combine oil, eggs, sugars, and applesauce and whisk together. Add carrots and stir until well combined.
5. Pour the wet ingredients into the dry. Stir until combined but take care not to over mix. Pour the batter evenly between the two cake pans. Bake for about 35 minutes in your Grill, rotating the cake pans halfway between the cook. Remove once a toothpick is inserted in the middle of the cake and comes out clean.
6. While the cake is cooling, prepare the frosting. Beat the cream cheese until smooth with a hand mixer. Add the butter and icing sugar and mix until fully combined.
7. On a clean plate or cake stand, place one half of the cake and top with a good layer of cream cheese frosting. Place the second half on top and cover with the remaining frosting. Icing tip: try not to lift your knife while icing. Instead make long, smooth strokes. Lifting the knife often make cause crumbs to get into your icing. Top with pecans if desired.

Chocolate Peanut Cookies

Servings: 4

Cooking Time: 12 Minutes

Ingredients:

- 1/2 Tsp Baking Soda
- 1/2 Cup Brown Sugar
- 1/2 Cup + 1 Tbsp Butter, Unsalted
- 1/3 Cup Cocoa Powder, Dark And Unsweetened
- 2 Eggs, Beaten
- 1 1/2 Cups Flour, All-Purpose
- 1/3 Cup Miniature Chocolate Chips
- 2 Cups Peanut Butter Chips, Divided
- 1/4 Tsp Sea Salt
- 1/2 Cup Sugar, Granulated
- 1 Tsp Vanilla Extract

Directions:

1. Supply your smoker with wood pellets and follow the start-up procedure. Preheat the grill, with the lid closed, to medium-low heat. If using a gas or charcoal grill, preheat a cast iron skillet.
2. In a mixing bowl, whisk together the flour, cocoa powder, baking soda, and salt. Set aside.
3. Set a metal saucepan on the griddle, then add ½ cup of butter to melt. Whisk in the sugars and vanilla extract and cook for 2 minutes. Remove the pan from the griddle, and transfer contents to a large mixing bowl.
4. Slowly pour the beaten eggs into the sugar mixture, whisking constantly to temper the eggs.
5. Add the dry mixture to the wet ingredients until just combined. Fold in 1 cup of peanut butter chips and chocolate chips. Refrigerate mixture for 15 to 30 minutes.
6. Remove the dough from the refrigerator, then add an additional cup of peanut butter chips.
7. Portion dough into 16 to 18 cookie balls.
8. Melt 1 tablespoon of butter on the griddle, then transfer the cookie balls to the griddle. Press down gently on the cookies, then cook for 10 to 12 minutes, flipping halfway.
9. Transfer cookies to a cooling rack for 5 minutes before enjoying.

Sourdough Pizza

Servings: 4

Cooking Time: 12 Minutes

Ingredients:
- 1 1/2 Cup Fresh Sourdough Starter
- 1 Tablespoon olive oil
- 1 Teaspoon Jacobsen Salt Co. Pure Kosher Sea Salt
- 1 1/4 Cup all-purpose flour

Directions:

1. Supply your smoker with wood pellets and follow the start-up procedure. Preheat the grill, with the lid closed, to 450° F.

2. Mix together the fresh sourdough starter, one tablespoon of oil, Jacobsen salt and 1-1/4 cups of flour. Add more flour, a little at a time, as needed to form a pizza dough consistency.

3. Allow the dough to rest for 30 minutes, to allow for easier rolling. Roll the dough out into a circle, using a small amount of flour to prevent sticking.

4. Place on a pizza stone. Bake the crust for approximately 7 minutes Grill: 450 °F

5. Remove the crust from the grill; brush on remaining oil to prevent toppings from soaking into the crust. Add the desired toppings and return pizza to grill; bake until the crust browns and the cheese melts.

Savory Cheesecake With Bourbon Pecan Topping

Servings: 6   Cooking Time: 75 Minutes

Ingredients:

- Crust
- 12 ounce Oreos
- 6 ounce melted butter
- Filling
- 24 ounces cream cheese - room temperature
- 1 cup granulated sugar
- 3 tbs cornstarch
- 2 large eggs
- 2/3 cup heavy cream
- 1 tbs vanilla
- 1 1/2 tbs bourbon
- Topping
- 3 large eggs beaten
- 1/3 cup granulated sugar
- 1/3 cup brown sugar
- 8 tbsp corn syrup dark corn syrup recommended
- 2 tbsp bourbon
- 1/2 tbsp vanilla
- 1/8 tbsp salt
- 3/4 cup rough chopped pecans (smoked pecans recommended)

Directions:

1. Supply your smoker with wood pellets and follow the start-up procedure. Preheat the grill, with the lid closed, to 350 °F.
2. Wrap foil on the bottom and up the sides of a 9" spring-form pan (outside of pan).
3. Butter the bottom & insides of the pan.
4. Crust
5. Throw ingredients in a food processor until they are finely ground.
6. Spread in 9" cheesecake pan on bottom & about ½ way upsides.
7. Filling
8. Place 8 oz of cream cheese in mixer bowl with 1/3 of sugar & cornstarch.Mix until smooth andcreamy.
9. Add another 8 oz cream cheese andbeat until smooth, then add remaining cream cheese,beating until smooth.
10. Then mix in the rest of the sugar, bourbon & vanilla.
11. Add eggs one at a time beating well after each one.
12. Add the heavy cream and mix just until smooth. Reminder: Do not over mix.
13. Pour batter into the prepared crust.
14. Topping

15. Mix all together except pecans.
16. Sprinkle pecans on top of cheesecake batter.
17. Pour topping over cheesecake batter.
18. Place in a pan big enough to hold a spring-form pan. Pour boiling water in the roasting pan to come up about ½ way up the spring-form pan.
19. Bake at 350 °F for 75 minutes until the top just barely jiggles. Carefully take the pan out of water-bath and put on cooling rack.
20. Let cool for 2 hours in pan. After 2 hours put in fridge until totally chilled then serve.

Baked Cast Iron Berry Cobbler

| Servings: 6 | Cooking Time: 35 Minutes |

Ingredients:

- 4 Cup Berries
- 12 Tablespoon sugar
- Cup orange juice
- 2/3 Cup Flour
- 3/4 Teaspoon baking powder
- 1 Pinch salt
- 1/2 Cup butter
- 1 Tablespoon Sugar, raw

Directions:

1. Supply your smoker with wood pellets and follow the start-up procedure. Preheat the grill, with the lid closed, to 350° F.
2. In a 10-inch (25-cm) cast iron or other baking pan, mix together the berries, 4 Tbsp sugar and the orange juice.
3. In a small bowl, mix together the flour, baking powder and salt. Set aside.
4. In a separate bowl, cream together the butter and granulated sugar. Add the egg and vanilla extract and mix to combine. Gradually fold in the flour mixture.
5. Spoon the batter on top of the berries and sprinkle raw sugar on top.
6. Bake the cobbler for approximately 35-45 minutes. Cool slightly and serve with whipped cream. Enjoy! Grill: 350 °F

Grilled Beer Cheese Dip

Servings: 6

Cooking Time: 20 Minutes

Ingredients:

- 6 Oz Beer, Can
- 8 Oz Cream Cheese
- 1 Tsp Onion Powder
- ½ Tsp Pepper
- ½ Tsp Salt
- 2 Cups Shredded Cheese

Directions:

1. Supply your smoker with wood pellets and follow the start-up procedure. Preheat the grill, with the lid closed, to 350° F. If you're using a gas or charcoal grill, set it up for medium high heat. Preheat with lid closed for 10-15 minutes.

2. In the cast iron pan add cream cheese, shredded cheese, beer, onion powder, salt and pepper. Once grill is at 350°F place cast iron skillet onto the grill and cook for about 10 minutes, stir and cook for another 5-10 minutes.

3. Top with more shredded cheese and fresh parsley. Serve with fresh baked pretzels as well.

Sweet Cheese Muffins

Servings: 3
Cooking Time: 15 Minutes

Ingredients:
- 1 package butter cake mix
- 1 package Jiffy Corn Muffin Mix
- 1 cup self-rising or cake flour
- 12 tablespoons (1½ sticks) unsalted butter, softened, plus 8 tablespoons (1 stick) melted
- 3½ cups shredded Cheddar cheese
- 2 eggs, beaten, at room temperature
- 2¼ cups buttermilk
- Nonstick cooking spray or butter, for greasing
- ¼ cup packed brown sugar

Directions:
1. Supply your smoker with wood pellets and follow the start-up procedure. Preheat, with the lid closed, to 375°F.
2. In a large mixing bowl, combine the cake mix, corn muffin mix, and flour.
3. Slice the 1½ sticks of softened butter into pieces and cut into the dry ingredients. Add the cheese and mix thoroughly.
4. In a medium bowl, combine the eggs and buttermilk, then add to the dry ingredients, stirring until well blended.
5. Coat three 12-cup mini muffin pans with cooking spray and spoon ¼ cup of batter into each cup.
6. Transfer the pans to the grill, close the lid, and smoke, monitoring closely, for 12 to 15 minutes, or until the muffins are lightly browned.
7. While the muffins are cooking, make the topping: In a small bowl, stir together the remaining 1 stick of melted butter and the brown sugar until well combined.
8. Remove the muffins from the grill. Brush the tops with the sweet butter and serve warm.

Garlic Cheese Pull Apart Bread

Servings: 2

Cooking Time: 20 Minutes

Ingredients:

- 1 Loaf Bread, Sourdough Round
- 2 1/2 Tbsp Butter, Salted
- 8 Oz Fontina Cheese
- 1 Grated Garlic, Roasted
- 1/4 Cup Parsley, Minced Fresh
- 1 Tsp Red Flakes Pepper
- 1 Pinch Salt

Directions:

1. Start your Grill on "smoke" with the lid open until a fire is established in the burn pot (3-7 minutes). Supply your smoker with wood pellets and follow the start-up procedure. Preheat the grill, with the lid closed, to 300° F.

2. In a small bowl, add the soft butter, grated garlic, red pepper flakes, sea salt, and ¼ cup of the chopped parsley, and whisk together. With a bread serrated knife, cut 1-inch slices into the bread, not cutting all the way through the bottom of the load. With a butter knife, spread a thin layer of the butter mixture on each slice of the bread. Take the serrated knife again, and cut across the loaf to form 1 inch squares. Next, slice the cheese into small thin slices, then stuff one slice into each bread opening. Place the bread on a baking sheet, and cover tightly with aluminum foil. Place on the grill for about 10 minutes, remove the foil, and grill for a few more minutes until the top is nicely golden and the cheese is oozing. Remove from the grill, sprinkle with fresh parsley leaves, then serve.

Baked Buttermilk Biscuits

Servings: 4

Cooking Time: 15 Minutes

Ingredients:

- 2 Cup all-purpose flour
- 1/4 Cup butter
- 3/4 Cup buttermilk

Directions:

1. Supply your smoker with wood pellets and follow the start-up procedure. Preheat the grill, with the lid closed, to High heat. Spoon the flour into a measuring cup and level with a knife.
2. Put the flour into a mixing bowl. Using a pastry blender, cut the butter into the flour until the mixture resembles coarse crumbs.
3. With a fork, gently stir in just enough of the buttermilk so the dough leaves the sides of the bowl. (You may not need all the buttermilk.) For the most tender biscuits, do not overmix.
4. Lightly flour a work surface as well as your hands. Tip the dough onto the floured surface and gently bring together using your fingertips. (Re-flour your hands or the board if the dough is too sticky.) Knead two or three times, just to bring the dough together.
5. With a floured rolling pin, lightly and quickly roll the dough out to a thickness of about 1/2". Using a 1-1/2" floured cutter, cut out as many biscuits as you can. (Do not twist the cutter; push it straight down.) You can reroll the scraps if desired, but the "second string" biscuits will be tougher.
6. Transfer the biscuits to an ungreased baking sheet. Using a pastry brush, brush the tops with melted butter. Bake until golden brown, 10 to 15 minutes. Enjoy! Grill: 500 °F

The Dan Patrick Show Pull-apart Pesto Bread

Servings: 8

Cooking Time: 25 Minutes

Ingredients:

- 1 Sourdough Bread, loaf
- 1/2 Cup butter, melted
- 1 Cup Pesto Sauce
- 1 1/2 Cup Italian Cheese Blend

Directions:

1. Supply your smoker with wood pellets and follow the start-up procedure. Preheat the grill, with the lid closed, to 350° F.
2. Using a serrated knife, make 1" diagonal cuts through the bread leaving the bottom crust intact. Turn the bread and make diagonal cuts in the opposite direction, creating diamonds.
3. Place the bread on a sheet of foil large enough to wrap around the entire loaf. Pour the melted butter into the cracks in the bread. Using a spoon spread the pesto into the cracks then follow with the cheese stuffing it down into each crack.
4. Fold up the edges of the foil to wrap up the loaf and transfer to a baking sheet. Place the baking sheet directly on the grill grate.
5. Bake for 15 minutes then unwrap the foil and cook for an additional 10 minutes. Remove from the grill and serve. Enjoy! Grill: 350 °F
6. Follow along as we give you a recipe each day this week from The Dan Patrick Show Game Day Recipes eBook.

Baked Wood-fired Pizza

Servings: 6 Cooking Time: 12 Minutes

Ingredients:

- 2/3 Cup warm water (110°F to 115°F)
- 2 1/2 Teaspoon active dry yeast
- 1/2 Teaspoon granulated sugar
- 1 Teaspoon kosher salt
- 1 Tablespoon oil
- 2 Cup all-purpose flour
- 1/4 Cup fine cornmeal
- 1 Large grilled portobello mushroom, sliced
- 1 Jar pickled artichoke hearts, drained and chopped
- 1 Cup shredded fontina cheese
- 1/2 Cup shaved Parmigiano-Reggiano cheese, divided
- To Taste Roasted Garlic, minced
- 1/4 Cup extra-virgin olive oil
- To Taste banana peppers

Directions:

1. In a glass bowl, stir together the warm water, yeast and sugar. Let stand until the mixture starts to foam, about 10 minutes. In a mixer, combine 1-3/4 cup flour, sugar and salt. Stir oil into the yeast mixture. Slowly add the liquid to the dry ingredients while slowly increasing the mixers speed until fully combined. The dough should be smooth and not sticky.
2. Knead the dough on a floured surface, gradually adding the remaining flour as needed to prevent the dough from sticking, until smooth, about 5 to 10 minutes.
3. Form the dough into a ball. Apply a thin layer of olive oil to a large bowl. Place the dough into the bowl and coat the dough ball with a small amount of olive oil. Cover and let rise in a warm place for about 1 hour or until doubled in size.
4. When ready to cook, set smoker temperature to 450°F and preheat, lid closed for 15 minutes.
5. Place a pizza stone in the grill while it preheats.
6. Punch the dough down and roll it out into a 12-inch circle on a floured surface.
7. Spread the cornmeal evenly on the pizza peel. Place the dough on the pizza peel and assemble the toppings evenly in the following order: olive oil, roasted garlic, fontina, portobello, artichoke hearts, Parmigiano-Reggiano and banana peppers.
8. Carefully slide the assembled pizza from the pizza peel to the preheated pizza stone and bake until the crust is golden brown, about 10 to 12 minutes. Enjoy!

Basil Margherita Pizza

Servings: 6

Cooking Time: 25 Minutes

Ingredients:

- Basil, Chopped
- 2 Cups Flour, All-Purpose
- Mozzarella Cheese, Sliced Rounds
- 1 Cup Pizza Sauce
- 1 Teaspoon Salt
- 1 Teaspoon Sugar
- 1 Tomato, Sliced
- 1 Cup Water, Warm
- 1 Teaspoon Yeast, Instant

Directions:

1. Combine the water, yeast, and sugar in a small bowl and let sit for about 5 minutes.
2. In a large bowl, stir together the flour and salt. Pour in the yeast mixture and mix until a soft dough forms. Knead for about 2 minutes. Place in an oiled bowl and cover with a cloth. Let the dough sit and rise for about 45 minutes or until the dough has doubled in size.
3. Roll out on a flat, floured surface (or on a pizza stone) until you"ve reached your desired shape and thickness.
4. Supply your smoker with wood pellets and follow the start-up procedure. Preheat the grill, with the lid closed, to 350° F.
5. On the rolled out dough, pour on the pizza sauce, cheese, and then tomatoes and basil. Place in your Grill and bake for about 25 minutes, or until the cheese is melted and slightly golden brown.

Cornbread Chicken Stuffing

Servings: 6 - 8

Cooking Time: 95 Minutes

Ingredients:
- 2 Tbsp Butter
- 1 Cup Chicken Stock
- 6 Cups Cornbread, Cubed
- ½ Cup Dried Cranberries
- 1 Egg
- ½ Cup Heavy Whipping Cream
- 1 Lb. Italian Sausage
- 1 Diced Onion
- 1 ½ Tsp Pulled Pork Rub
- 2 Tbsp Sage, Fresh
- ½ Tsp Fresh Thyme

Directions:

1. Supply your smoker with wood pellets and follow the start-up procedure. Preheat the grill, with the lid closed, to 250° F. If using a gas or charcoal grill, set the temp to low heat.
2. Portion sausage into quarter-size pieces and place on mesh grate. Place grate on the grill and cook for 1 hour. Sausage pieces will have a smoky deep brown color. Move the mesh tray of sausage to the side of the grill with indirect heat.
3. Open the Flame Broiler Plate and increase the temperature to 350°F. Place a large cast iron skillet on the grill, over direct flame. Add butter and onions and cook until the onions caramelize lightly, stirring often. Add the sage and thyme and stir to combine.
4. Gently fold in the dried cranberries and cubed cornbread, then add sausage directly from mesh grate.
5. In a small mixing bowl, whisk together the heavy cream, chicken stock, egg, and Pulled Pork Rub. Pour mixture over the cornbread stuffing mix.
6. Cover grill and cook 30 minutes or until heated through and crispy on top.

Chocolate Lava Cake With Smoked Whipped Cream

Servings: 4   Cooking Time: 45 Minutes

Ingredients:

- 1 Pint heavy whipping cream
- 9 Tablespoon Butter
- 220 G Semisweet Chocolate
- 1 1/4 Cup powdered sugar
- 2 Large eggs
- 2 egg yolk
- 6 Tablespoon flour
- 1 Tablespoon Bourbon Vanilla
- Powdered Sugar
- cocoa powder

Directions:

1. Supply your smoker with wood pellets and follow the start-up procedure. Preheat the grill, with the lid closed, to 180° F.
2. For the Smoked Whipped Cream: Add cream to a shallow, aluminum baking pan. Place the pan on the grill and smoke for 30 minutes.
3. Pour the smoked cream into a large mixing bowl and refrigerate for later use. Grill: 180 °F
4. Increase the grill temperature to 375°F and preheat. Grill: 375 °F
5. Brush 4 small soufflé cups with 1 tablespoon melted butter.
6. Melt the chocolate and remaining butter in a heatproof bowl over simmering water, stir until smooth.
7. Stir in powdered sugar. Add eggs and egg yolks, stirring continuously. Whisk in flour until blended completely.
8. Pour batter into the prepared soufflé cups. Place them on the Traeger and bake for 13-14 minutes, or until the sides are set. Grill: 375 °F
9. For the Whipped Cream: Remove the chilled smoked cream from the refrigerator, add the bourbon vanilla and whip until airy.
10. Add confectioners sugar and continue whipping until whipped cream forms stiff peaks.
11. Dust lava cakes with confectioners sugar and cocoa, top with a dollop of smoke-infused whipped cream. Enjoy!

PORK RECIPES

Smoky Pork Tenderloin

Servings: 4
Cooking Time: 20 Minutes

Ingredients:
- 2 Pork Tenderloins (3-5 Pounds Total), Trimmed of Excess Fat or Silver Skin
- 1 Tablespoon Olive Oil
- 1-2 Tablespoons Fresh Lime Juice
- 1/4 Cup Light Brown Sugar
- 2 Teaspoons Smoked Paprika
- 1 Teaspoon Onion Powder
- 1 Teaspoon Garlic Powder
- 1 Teaspoon Coarse, Kosher Salt
- Pinch of Coarsely Ground Black Pepper

Directions:
1. Stir together the olive oil, lime juice, brown sugar, paprika, onion powder, garlic powder, salt, and pepper in a small bowl.
2. Rub the mixture over the pork and place the meat in a shallow dish. You can grill right away, but for more flavor, cover the dish and refrigerate up to 24 hours.
3. Supply your smoker with wood pellets and follow the start-up procedure. Preheat the grill, with the lid closed, to 375° F.
4. Grill the pork tenderloin for 10 minutes, flip and continue to cook until internal temperature at the thickest part of the meat registers 145 degrees F on an instant-read thermometer, about 8-10 minutes.
5. Remove the pork from the grill and cover with aluminum foil for 10-15 minutes before slicing and serving.

Smoked Bbq Ribs

Servings: 4

Cooking Time: 300 Minutes

Ingredients:

- 2 Rack St. Louis-style ribs
- 1/4 Cup Big Game Rub
- 1 Cup apple juice
- BBQ Sauce

Directions:

1. Pat ribs dry and peel the membrane from the back of the ribs.
2. Apply an even coat of rub to the front, back and sides of the ribs. Let sit for 20 minutes and up to 4 hours if refrigerated.
3. Supply your smoker with wood pellets and follow the start-up procedure. Preheat the grill, with the lid closed, to 225° F.
4. Place ribs, bone side down on grill. Put apple juice in a spray bottle and spray the ribs after 1 hour of cooking. Spray every 45 minutes thereafter. Grill: 225 °F Probe: 201 °F
5. After 4-1/2 hours, check the internal temperature of ribs. Ribs are done when internal temperature reaches 201°F. If not, check back in another 30 minutes. Grill: 225 °F Probe: 201 °F
6. Once ribs are done, brush a light layer of your favorite Traeger BBQ Sauce on the front and back of the ribs. Let the sauce set for 10 minutes. After the sauce has set, take ribs off the grill and let rest for 10 minutes. Slice ribs in between the bones and serve with extra sauce. Enjoy!

Smoked Porchetta With Italian Salsa Verde

Servings: 8-12   Cooking Time: 180 Minutes

Ingredients:

- 3 Tablespoon dried fennel seed
- 2 Tablespoon red pepper flakes
- 2 Tablespoon sage, minced
- 1 Tablespoon rosemary, minced
- 3 Clove garlic, minced
- As Needed lemon zest
- As Needed orange zest
- To Taste salt and pepper
- 6 Pound Pork Belly, skin on
- As Needed salt and pepper
- 1 Whole shallot, thinly sliced
- 6 Tablespoon parsley, minced
- 2 Tablespoon freshly minced chives
- 1 Tablespoon Oregano, fresh
- 3 Tablespoon white wine vinegar
- 1/2 Teaspoon kosher salt
- 3/4 Cup olive oil
- 1/2 Teaspoon Dijon mustard
- As Needed fresh lemon juice

Directions:

1. Prepare herb mixture: In a medium bowl, mix together fennel seeds, red pepper flakes, sage, rosemary, garlic, citrus zest, salt and pepper.
2. Place pork belly skin side up on a clean work surface and score in a crosshatch pattern. Flip the pork belly over and season flesh side with salt, pepper and half of the herb mixture.
3. Place trimmed pork loin in the center of the belly and rub with remaining herb mixture. Season with salt and pepper.
4. Roll the pork belly around the loin to form a cylindrical shape and tie tightly with kitchen twine at 1" intervals.
5. Season the outside with salt and pepper and transfer to refrigerator, uncovered and let air dry overnight.
6. When ready to cook, start the smoker grill and set to Smoke.
7. Fit a rimmed baking sheet with a rack and place the pork on the rack seam side down.
8. Place the pan directly on the grill grate and smoke for 1 hour.
9. Increase the grill temperature to 325 degrees F and roast until the internal temperature of the meat reaches 135 degrees, about 2 1/2 hours. If the exterior begins to burn before the desired internal temperature is reached, tent with foil.
10. Remove from grill and let stand 30 minutes before slicing.
11. To make the Italian salsa verde: Combine shallot, parsley, chives, vinegar, oregano and salt in a medium bowl. Whisk in olive oil then stir in mustard and lemon juice.
12. Drizzle slices with Italian salsa verde and enjoy!

Smoked Traeger Pulled Pork

Servings: 8

Cooking Time: 540 Minutes

Ingredients:

- 1 (6-9 lb) bone-in pork shoulder
- Pork & Poultry Rub
- 2 Cup apple cider
- 'Que BBQ Sauce

Directions:

1. Supply your smoker with wood pellets and follow the start-up procedure. Preheat the grill, with the lid closed, to 250° F.
2. While the Traeger comes to temperature, trim excess fat off pork butt.
3. Generously season with Traeger Pork & Poultry Rub on all sides and let sit for 20 minutes.
4. Place the pork butt fat side up directly on the grill grate and cook until the internal temperature reaches 160°F, about 3 to 5 hours. Grill: 250 °F Probe: 160 °F
5. Remove the pork butt from the grill.
6. On a large baking sheet, stack 4 large pieces of aluminum foil on top of each other, ensuring they are wide enough to wrap the pork butt entirely on all sides. If not, overlap the foil pieces to create a wider base. Place the pork butt in the center on the foil, then bring up the sides of the foil a little bit before pouring the apple cider on top of the pork butt. Wrap the foil tightly around the pork, ensuring the cider does not escape.
7. Place the foil-wrapped pork butt back on the grill fat side up and cook until the internal temperature reaches 204°F, in the thickest part of the meat, about 3 to 4 hours longer depending on the size of the pork butt. Grill: 250 °F Probe: 204 °F
8. Remove from the grill. Allow the pork to rest for 45 minutes in the foil packet.
9. Remove the pork from the foil and pour off any excess liquid into a fat separator.
10. Place the pork in a large dish and shred the meat, removing and discarding the bone and any excess fat. Add separated liquid back into pork and season to taste with additional Traeger Big Game Rub. Optionally, add Traeger 'Que BBQ Sauce or your favorite BBQ sauce to taste.

Double Smoked Apple Spiral Ham

Servings: 12

Cooking Time: 150 Minutes

Ingredients:
- 1 10 lb ham spiral cut
- 1 cup apple jelly
- 1 cup raspberry chipotle BBQ sauce

Directions:
1. Supply your smoker with wood pellets and follow the start-up procedure. Preheat the grill, with the lid closed, to 275° F.
2. Remove ham from all packaging and transfer to a chicken tray, cut-side-down. Then place on a cooking tray and transfer to the smoker. Close the lid and cook for 2 hours.
3. Heat up saucepan over medium heat. Add apple jelly and stir well, until it reaches a liquid consistency.
4. Add raspberry chipotle. Stir in and bring glaze to a simmer. Leave saucepan on warm heat until ham is ready.
5. After two hours, transfer ham to a shallow aluminum pan. Apply the glaze to ham generously using a basting brush. Make sure all cracks on ham surfaceare glazed.
6. Still in a shallow pan, put ham back in smoker. Close the lid and leave to smoke for over 30 minutes.
7. Remove ham from smoker and transfer to a cutting board. Leave to rest for 10 minutes.
8. Cut along the outer seam of the ham, allowing the slices to fall away.

Bbq Pulled Pork Grilled Cheese Sandwich

Servings: 8 Cooking Time: 540 Minutes

Ingredients:

- 1 Pork Butt, bone-in, 8-10 lbs.
- 2 Tablespoon Pork & Poultry Rub
- 1 1/2 Cup apple juice
- 4 Tablespoon brown sugar
- 1 Tablespoon salt
- Sweet & Heat BBQ Sauce
- 16 Pieces White Bread
- cheddar cheese
- butter, softened

Directions:

1. Trim pork butt of all excess fat leaving 1/4-inch of the fat cap attached.
2. Combine 2 Tbsp Traeger Pork & Poultry Rub, apple juice, brown sugar and salt in a small bowl stirring until most of the sugar and salt are dissolved.
3. Inject the pork butt every square inch or so with the apple juice mixture. Season the exterior of the pork butt with remaining rub.
4. Supply your smoker with wood pellets and follow the start-up procedure. Preheat the grill, with the lid closed, to 250° F.
5. Place pork butt directly on the grill grate and cook for about 6 hours or until the internal temperature reaches 160 degrees F. Remove pork butt from grill and wrap in two layers of foil. Pour in 1/2 cup of apple juice. Secure tin foil tightly to contain the apple juice. Grill: 250 °F Probe: 160 °F
6. Increase temperature to 275 degrees F and return to grill in a pan large enough to hold the pork butt in case of leaks. Cook an additional 3 hours or until internal temperature reaches 205 degrees F. Grill: 275 °F Probe: 205 °F
7. Remove from the grill and discard the bone. Shred the pork removing any excess fat or tendons. Season with additional Traeger Pork & Poultry Rub and salt if needed. Add Traeger Sweet & Heat BBQ Sauce and mix to combine. Set pork aside.
8. For the grilled cheese sandwiches: Butter two pieces of bread and place one in a pan warmed over medium heat, butter side down. Place a slice of cheddar cheese on top of the bread and top with pulled pork. Place another slice of cheese on top of pork and finish with the other slice of bread, butter side up.
9. Cook on first side 5-7 minutes until bread is lightly browned. Flip and cook for another 5-7 minutes. Remove from heat and slice in half. Enjoy!

Traeger Smoked Sausage

Servings: 4

Cooking Time: 120 Minutes

Ingredients:
- 3 Pound ground pork
- 1/2 Tablespoon ground mustard
- 1 Tablespoon onion powder
- 1 Tablespoon garlic powder
- 1/2 Teaspoon pink curing salt
- 1 Tablespoon salt
- 4 Teaspoon black pepper
- 1/2 Cup ice water
- Hog casings, soaked and rinsed in cold water

Directions:
1. In a medium bowl, combine the meat and seasonings, mix well.
2. Add ice water to meat and mix with hands working quickly until everything is incorporated.
3. Place mixture in a sausage stuffer and follow manufacturers Directions:for operating. Use caution not to overstuff or the casing might burst.
4. Once all the meat is stuffed, determine your desired link length and pinch and twist a couple of times or tie it off. Repeat for each link.
5. Supply your smoker with wood pellets and follow the start-up procedure. Preheat the grill, with the lid closed, to 225° F.
6. Place links directly on the grill grate and cook for 1 to 2 hours or until the internal temperature registers 155°F. Let sausage rest a few minutes before slicing. Enjoy! Grill: 225 °F Probe: 155 °F

Pork Tenderloin

Servings: 2

Cooking Time: 15 Minutes

Ingredients:

- 1 Pound pork tenderloin
- 1/3 Cup Kentucky bourbon or apple juice
- 1/4 Cup low sodium soy sauce
- 1/4 Cup brown sugar, packed
- 2 Tablespoon Dijon mustard
- 2 Teaspoon Worcestershire sauce
- 1 Teaspoon ground black pepper
- 1 Medium onion, chopped
- 2 Clove garlic, minced

Directions:

1. Trim any silverskin from the tenderloins with a sharp knife. Place meat in a large resealable plastic bag.
2. For the marinade: In a small mixing bowl or resealable bag, combine the bourbon, soy sauce, brown sugar, mustard, Worcestershire sauce and pepper, whisk to mix. Stir in the onion and garlic. Pour over the tenderloins and refrigerate for 8 hours or overnight.
3. Supply your smoker with wood pellets and follow the start-up procedure. Preheat the grill, with the lid closed, to 400° F.
4. Remove the pork from the marinade and scrape off any solid ingredients (onion or bits of garlic). Discard the marinade.
5. Arrange the tenderloins on the grill grate and grill for 6 to 8 minutes per side or until the internal temperature is 145°F. The pork will still be slightly pink in the center. If you prefer your pork well-done, cook it to 160°F. Grill: 400 °F Probe: 145 °F
6. Transfer the tenderloins to a cutting board. Let rest for several minutes before carving on a diagonal into 1/2 inch slices. Enjoy!

Pig On A Stick With Buffalo Glaze

Servings: 12   Cooking Time: 75 Minutes

Ingredients:

- 4lb (1.8kg) pork shanks, each about 4 to 6oz (110 to 170g), trimmed and thawed if frozen
- 1½ cups sugar-free dark-colored soda, sugar-free root beer, or no-sugar-added apple juice
- for the brine (optional)
- 1 gallon (3.8 liters) distilled water
- ¾ cup kosher salt
- 5 tsp pink curing salt #1
- for the glaze (optional)
- ½ cup unsalted butter
- 1 cup hot sauce
- 2 tsp granulated garlic
- 1 tsp Worcestershire sauce

Directions:

1. In a stockpot on the stovetop over medium-high heat, make the brine by combining the ingredients and bringing the mixture to a boil. Stir until the salts dissolve. Remove the pot from the stovetop and let the brine cool to room temperature.
2. Add the pork shanks to the brine. Cover and refrigerate for 2 days.
3. Supply your smoker with wood pellets and follow the start-up procedure. Preheat the grill, with the lid closed, to 180° F.
4. Drain the pork shanks and discard the brine. (If you didn't brine the pork shanks, season them on all sides with your favorite barbecue rub.) Place the pork on the grate and smoke for 3 hours. Transfer the shanks to an aluminum roasting pan.
5. Raise the temperature to 275°F (135°C).
6. Add the soda to the pan and cover tightly with aluminum foil. Place the pan on the grate and braise the meat until it's tender but still attached to the bone, about 2 to 3 hours. Be careful when removing the foil because steam will escape. Remove the pan from the grill and set aside.
7. Raise the temperature to 325°F (163°C).
8. In a saucepan on the stovetop over medium heat, make the buffalo glaze by melting the butter. Stir in the remaining ingredients. Let the sauce simmer for 5 minutes to allow the flavors to blend.
9. Dip the pork shanks into the glaze and then transfer them to an aluminum foil roasting pan. Cover tightly with aluminum foil. Place the pan on the grate and cook the shanks until hot, about 30 minutes.
10. Remove the pan from the grill. Serve the pork with plenty of napkins.

Egg Bacon French Toast Panini

Servings: 2

Cooking Time: 10 Minutes

Ingredients:
- 6 Bacon Slices
- 1 Tbsp Black Pepper
- 4 Brioche Sandwich Slices, Day Old
- 2 Tbsp Butter
- 1 Tbsp Cinnamon-Sugar
- 6 Eggs
- 1 Tbsp Heavy Cream
- 1 Tbsp Maple Syrup
- 1 Tbsp Salt

Directions:

1. Supply your smoker with wood pellets and follow the start-up procedure. Preheat the grill, with the lid open, to 375° F. If using a gas or charcoal grill, set heat to medium heat. For all other grills, preheat cast iron skillet on grill grates.
2. Place butter on griddle and spread to coat surface.
3. In a pie plate, whisk together 2 eggs, heavy cream, and maple syrup.
4. Soak both sides of bread slices in egg mixture and transfer to griddle. Cook for 2 minutes, flipping halfway until egg mixture is cooked and golden. Set aside.
5. Lay bacon on the griddle, and cook 3 minutes per side, until golden.
6. Transfer to lower right-hand corner of griddle to keep warm.
7. Crack 4 eggs on top of rendered bacon fat. Season with salt and pepper. Cook 1 minute per side, or to desired doneness.
8. Lay eggs on top of French toast, add bacon, then place the other slice of French Toast on top.
9. Transfer back to griddle for another minute to warm, sprinkle with extra cinnamon-sugar, then slice in half and serve hot.

Bacon Grilled Cheese Sandwich

Servings: 4

Cooking Time: 10 Minutes

Ingredients:

- mayonnaise
- 8 Slices Texas toast
- 16 Slices cheddar cheese
- 1 Pound applewood smoked bacon slices, cooked
- butter, softened

Directions:

1. Supply your smoker with wood pellets and follow the start-up procedure. Preheat the grill, with the lid closed, to 350° F.
2. Spread a little bit of mayonnaise on each piece of bread.
3. Place 1 piece of cheddar cheese on bread slice then top with a couple slices of bacon. Add another slice of cheese then top with the other piece of bread. Spread softened butter on the exterior of the top piece of bread.
4. When the grill is hot, place the grilled cheese directly on a cleaned, oiled grill grate buttered side down. Spread softened butter on the exterior of the top slice. Grill: 350 °F
5. Cook the grilled cheese on the first side for 5 to 7 minutes until grill marks develop and the cheese has begun to melt. Flip the sandwich and repeat on the other side. Grill: 350 °F
6. Remove from the grill when the cheese is melted and the exterior is lightly toasted. Enjoy!

Bbq Pulled Coleslaw Pork Sandwiches

Servings: 12

Cooking Time: 480 Minutes

Ingredients:

- 1 Bottle Bbq Sauce
- Coleslaw, Prepared
- 12 Kaiser Rolls
- 8-10Lbs Pork Butt Roast, Bone-In
- 5 Oz Sugar
- 1 Cup Yellow Mustard

Directions:

1. Supply your smoker with wood pellets and follow the start-up procedure. Preheat the grill, with the lid open, to 225° F. While your grill is heating, remove the pork roast from its packaging and place on a cookie sheet. Rub the pork roast down with yellow mustard.

2. Mix BBQ sauce and sugar in a bowl. Rub the roast down with entire mixture, allowing time for the rub to melt into the meat.

3. Place the roast in the smoker and cook for 6 hours.

4. After 6 hours, remove the roast and double wrap in tin foil. Turn the grill up to 250°F and cook the roast for another 2 hours or until the roast is probe tender (around an internal temperature of 204°F). Let the pork butt rest in the foil for up to an hour before pulling.

5. Cut each Kaiser roll in half, mix pulled pork with some more barbecue sauce and pile on each half of roll. Top with coleslaw and green onions. Don't mix all the pulled pork with barbecue sauce so that you can use the extra pulled pork for different recipes. Serve hot and enjoy!

Smoked Ribs

Servings: 4

Cooking Time: 315 Minutes

Ingredients:
- 2 Racks Baby Back Rib
- Sweet Rib Rub

Directions:

1. Supply your smoker with wood pellets and follow the start-up procedure. Preheat the grill, with the lid open, to 225° F.
2. Remove the membrane on the reverse side of the ribs by sliding a butter knife under the membrane and breaking it. With a piece of paper towel, grab the broken membrane and peel back until the entire membrane is removed.
3. Season both sides of the ribs with Sweet Rib Rub.
4. Place the ribs, meat side up, on the grates of the grill and close the lid. Smoke for about 4 1/2 hours.
5. Wrap in foil and return to the grill at 350°F for another 45 minutes.
6. Pull your ribs off the grill and rest for 10 minutes.
7. Slice and serve hot. Enjoy!

Roasted Pork With Balsamic Strawberry Sauce

Servings: 2

Cooking Time: 35 Minutes

Ingredients:

- 2 Pound pork tenderloin
- salt and pepper
- 2 Tablespoon dried rosemary
- 2 Tablespoon extra-virgin olive oil
- 12 Large fresh strawberries
- 1 Cup balsamic vinegar
- 4 Tablespoon sugar

Directions:

1. Supply your smoker with wood pellets and follow the start-up procedure. Preheat the grill, with the lid closed, to 350° F.
2. Rinse pork and pat dry. Sprinkle both sides with salt, pepper, and rosemary.
3. In a large Dutch oven skillet, heat oil on High until almost smoking. Add the tenderloin and sear on each side until the skin is golden brown, about 2 minutes per side.
4. Set the skillet in the Traeger and cook until pork is no longer pink and internal temperature reaches 150°F, about 20 minutes. Grill: 350 °F Probe: 150 °F
5. Remove from grill and let the pork rest for 5-10 minutes.
6. Add strawberries to the skillet over the stove on medium heat and quickly sear on both sides for less than a minute. Remove berries from the pan.
7. Add balsamic vinegar to the same pan and scrape the browned bits from the bottom.
8. Bring to a boil and then reduce heat to medium low. Add the sugar, stirring frequently. Sauce is ready when it has reduced by half and texture is thick.
9. Slice the pork and place the seared strawberries on top. Serve with a drizzle of the balsamic vinegar sauce. Enjoy!

POULTRY RECIPES

Oktoberfest Pretzel Mustard Chicken

Servings: 4
Cooking Time: 25 Minutes

Ingredients:
- 1/4 Pound pretzel sticks
- 3 Tablespoon Dijon mustard
- 3 Tablespoon apple cider or brown ale
- 1 Tablespoon honey
- 1 1/2 Teaspoon fresh thyme, plus more for garnish
- 4 boneless, skinless chicken breasts

Directions:
1. Pulse the pretzel sticks in a food processor or crush by hand in a resealable bag until they've turned into a powder the texture of panko breadcrumbs.
2. Transfer the crumbs to a wide, shallow bowl.
3. In separate shallow bowl, whisk mustard, beer or cider, honey and thyme together.
4. Spray a wire rack with cooking spray and place atop a sheet tray. Dip each chicken breast in the mustard mixture, then dredge in the pretzel crumbs to coat evenly and place on the wire rack. Spray the top of each chicken breast lightly with cooking spray.
5. Supply your smoker with wood pellets and follow the start-up procedure. Preheat the grill, with the lid closed, to 375° F.
6. Place the pan on the Traeger and bake for about 20 to 25 minutes, until the chicken breasts are fully cooked and register 165°F on an instant-read thermometer. Grill: 375 °F Probe: 165 °F
7. Let chicken rest for 5 minutes. Garnish with fresh thyme if desired. Enjoy!

Cheese Chicken Cordon Bleu

Servings: 8

Cooking Time: 75 Minutes

Ingredients:

- 8 Chicken, Boneless/Skinless
- 1 Cup Mozzarella Cheese, Shredded
- Lemon Pepper Garlic Seasoning
- 8 Prosciutto, Sliced

Directions:

1. Supply your smoker with wood pellets and follow the start-up procedure. Preheat the grill, with the lid closed, to 250° F.
2. Pound each chicken breast with a mallet or cast iron pan so that it's about ½ inch thick.
3. On a piece of prosciutto, sprinkle mozzarella cheese and roll up. Place in the middle of a chicken breast and wrap the chicken around the prosciutto roll. Sprinkle with Lemon Pepper seasoning.
4. Smoke for an hour to 75 minutes, or until internal temperature reaches 165 degrees F.

Grilled Beantown Chicken Wings

Servings: 8

Cooking Time: 50 Minutes

Ingredients:

- 3 Pound chicken wings
- 1/4 Cup vegetable oil
- 1 1/2 Tablespoon Pork & Poultry Rub
- 1 Cup Irish Stout
- 1/2 Cup butter
- 2 Tablespoon apple jelly
- 1 Cup Frank's RedHot Sauce

Directions:

1. Rinse the chicken wings under cold running water and pat dry. With a sharp knife, cut the wings into three pieces through the joints. Discard the wing tips, or save for chicken stock.
2. Transfer the remaining "drumettes" and "flats" to a large a bowl. Add the oil and the Traeger Pork and Poultry shake, and toss with your hands to coat the wings evenly.
3. Make the beer sauce: In a small saucepan, bring the beer to a boil over high heat and reduce by half. Reduce the heat to medium-low and add the butter, stirring until melted. Stir in the apple jelly and the hot sauce. Keep warm.
4. Supply your smoker with wood pellets and follow the start-up procedure. Preheat the grill, with the lid closed, to 350° F.
5. Arrange the wings on the grill grate. Cook for 45 to 50 minutes, or until the chicken is no longer pink at the bone, turning once halfway through. Transfer the wings to a large clean bowl and pour the beer sauce over the wings, tossing to coat. Serve immediately. Grill: 350 °F

Grilled Parmesan Chicken Wings

Servings: 4

Cooking Time: 25 Minutes

Ingredients:
- 4 Tbsp Butter
- 4 Lbs Chicken Wings, Trimmed And Patted Dry
- 4 Garlic Cloves, Chopped
- 2 Tbsp Olive Oil
- 1/2 Cup Parmesan Cheese, Grated
- 2 Tbsp Parsley, Chopped
- Champion Chicken Seasoning

Directions:
1. Lay chicken wings out on a sheet tray, blot with paper towel, then season with Champion Chicken.
2. Supply your smoker with wood pellets and follow the start-up procedure. Preheat the grill, with the lid open, to 400° F. If using a gas or charcoal grill, set it up for medium-high heat.
3. Transfer wings to grill and cook for 20 to 25 minutes, turning every 5 minutes, until lightly browned. Remove wings from the grill and set on a sheet tray. Place in the smoking cabinet to keep warm while preparing the garlic butter.
4. Melt butter and olive oil in a cast iron skillet, then add garlic and simmer until fragrant. Remove from the grill.
5. Transfer chicken wings to a large bowl and pour garlic butter over the wings. Add cheese and parsley, then toss well to coat. Serve warm with additional sprinkling of parmesan cheese.

Bbq Chicken Tostada

Servings: 4

Cooking Time: 50 Minutes

Ingredients:
- 4 Whole boneless, skinless chicken thighs
- salt and pepper
- 8 Whole Corn Tostada
- Refried Beans
- lettuce
- green onion, coarsely chopped
- cilantro, chopped
- guacamole

Directions:
1. Supply your smoker with wood pellets and follow the start-up procedure. Preheat the grill, with the lid closed, to 350° F.
2. While grill heats, trim excess fat and skin from chicken thighs.
3. Season with a light layer of salt and pepper.
4. Place chicken thighs on the grill grate and cook for 35 minutes.
5. Check internal temperature; chicken is done when a thermometer inserted reads 175 degrees F. Remove from the grill and let rest for 10 minutes before shredding.
6. Place tostadas on grill while chicken is resting for 5 minutes.
7. Build tostadas starting with refried beans, sliced lettuce, shredded chicken, tomatoes, green onions, cilantro, guacamole. Enjoy!

Green Goddess Chicken Legs

Servings: 4

Cooking Time: 40 Minutes

Ingredients:

- 2 Pound chicken legs
- 2 Cup Prepared "Green Goddess" Dressing
- 1/4 Cup parsley, chopped
- 1 Tablespoon paprika

Directions:

1. Place the chicken legs in a large resealable plastic bag. Combine the Green Goddess dressing as well as the parsley and paprika. Pour over the chicken legs. Refrigerate for 2 to 8 hours.

2. Supply your smoker with wood pellets and follow the start-up procedure. Preheat the grill, with the lid closed, to 350° F. Drain the chicken legs. Arrange the legs directly on the grill grate and grill, turning once, for 40 to 50 minutes, or until the legs are golden brown and cooked through. Serve at once. Grill: 350 °F

Savory Jerk Chicken Wings

Servings: 4

Cooking Time: 20 Minutes

Ingredients:

- 1 Tsp Allspice, Ground
- 3 Lbs Chicken Wings, Split
- 1/2 Tsp Cinnamon, Ground
- 4 Garlic Cloves, Smashed
- 2 Tsp Ginger, Grated
- 1 Habanero Pepper, Chopped
- 2 Tbsp Honey
- 2 Tbsp Lemon Juice
- 1/3 Cup Lime Juice
- 1/2 Tsp Nutmeg, Ground
- 1/2 Cup Olive Oil
- 1/4 Cup Poblano Pepper, Chopped
- 1 Tbsp Tamari
- 2 Tsp Thyme, Dried
- 1/2 Cup Yellow Onion, Chopped

Directions:

1. Add chicken to a large resealable plastic bag.
2. In the bowl of a food processor, add the garlic, onion, ginger, peppers, tamari, honey, lime juice, lemon juice, thyme, allspice, cinnamon, nutmeg, and oil. Process on low for 1 minute, then transfer marinade to the bag. Seal the bag and place in the refrigerator for at least 2 hours, up to overnight.
3. Supply your smoker with wood pellets and follow the start-up procedure. Preheat the grill, with the lid open, to 425° F. If using a gas or charcoal grill, set it up for medium-high heat.
4. Remove wings from the marinade, and discard remaining marinade. Place wings on the grill and cook for 15 to 20 minutes, flipping every 5 minutes, until an internal temperature of 165 F is reached.
5. Remove wings from the grill and serve warm.

Cheese Buffalo Chicken Wings

Servings: 4-6

Cooking Time: 25 Minutes

Ingredients:
- Bleu Cheese Dip
- ⅔ Cup Buffalo Sauce
- Celery
- 2 Lbs. Chicken Wings
- ½ Cup Sweet Heat Rub

Directions:

1. Supply your smoker with wood pellets and follow the start-up procedure. Preheat the grill, with the lid open, to 450° F. If using a gas or charcoal grill, set heat to high heat.
2. Rub wings generously with Sweet Heat Rub and transfer to wing rack.
3. Place rack on grill and cook for 20 minutes, rotating after 10 minutes.
4. Baste with sauce, then cover and grill an additional 5 to 7 minutes. Note: your cooking time will vary depending on the size of the wings. When done, wings should have an internal temperature of 165°F.
5. Remove wings from grill and transfer to a baking sheet and let rest for about 5 minutes.
6. Transfer wings to a large bowl and coat with the Buffalo Sauce. Shake the bowl around gently to combine or use a spatula to ensure every wing is coated.
7. Serve hot with extra sauce, celery, and bleu cheese dip.

Applewood-smoked Whole Turkey

Servings: 6-8

Cooking Time: 300 Minutes

Ingredients:
- 1 (10- to 12-pound) turkey, giblets removed
- Extra-virgin olive oil, for rubbing
- ¼ cup poultry seasoning
- 8 tablespoons (1 stick) unsalted butter, melted
- ½ cup apple juice
- 2 teaspoons dried sage
- 2 teaspoons dried thyme

Directions:
1. Supply your smoker with wood pellets and follow the start-up procedure. Preheat, with the lid closed, to 250°F.
2. Rub the turkey with oil and season with the poultry seasoning inside and out, getting under the skin.
3. In a bowl, combine the melted butter, apple juice, sage, and thyme to use for basting.
4. Put the turkey in a roasting pan, place on the grill, close the lid, and grill for 5 to 6 hours, basting every hour, until the skin is brown and crispy, or until a meat thermometer inserted in the thickest part of the thigh reads 165°F.
5. Let the bird rest for 15 to 20 minutes before carving.

Cajun Brined Maple Smoked Turkey Breast

Servings: 4

Cooking Time: 180 Minutes

Ingredients:

- 1 Gallon water
- 3/4 Cup canning and pickling salt
- 3 Tablespoon minced garlic
- 3 Tablespoon dark brown sugar
- 2 Tablespoon Worcestershire sauce
- 2 Tablespoon Cajun seasoning
- 1 (5-6 lb) bone-in turkey breast
- 3 Tablespoon extra-virgin olive oil
- 2 Tablespoon Cajun seasoning

Directions:

1. In a large food safe container or bucket, combine all of the ingredients for the brine with 1 gallon water. Stir until the salt is dissolved.
2. Place the turkey breast in the brine and weigh it down to ensure it is fully submerged. Cover and brine in a refrigerator for 1 to 2 days.
3. Remove the turkey breast from the brine and pat dry. Drizzle with the olive oil using your hands to cover all areas of the bird. Season liberally with Cajun seasoning. Probe: 165 °F
4. Supply your smoker with wood pellets and follow the start-up procedure. Preheat the grill, with the lid closed, to 225° F.
5. Place the turkey breast directly on the grill grate, close the lid and cook for 3 hours. After 3 hours, increase the temperature to 425°F and continue to cook for another 30 minutes or until the internal temperature reads 165°F when a thermometer is inserted into the thickest part of the breast. Grill: 225 °F Probe: 165 °F
6. Remove the turkey breast from the grill and allow to rest for at least 15 minutes before slicing. Slice and serve. Enjoy!

Cornish Game Hens

Servings: 4

Cooking Time: 60 Minutes

Ingredients:
- 4 Cornish game hens
- 4 Tablespoon butter, melted
- Chicken Rub
- 4 Sprig rosemary or sage, plus more for garnish

Directions:
1. Rinse the Cornish game hens under cold running water, inside and out. (Game hens do not usually come with giblets, but check the cavity for them before rinsing. If you find giblets, freeze them for chicken stock, if desired.)
2. Dry thoroughly with paper towels. Tuck the wings behind the backs and tie the legs together with butcher's string.
3. Rub the outside of each hen with the melted butter. Season with Traeger Chicken Rub. Slip a sprig of rosemary into the main cavity of each hen.
4. Supply your smoker with wood pellets and follow the start-up procedure. Preheat the grill, with the lid closed, to 375° F.
5. Roast the hens for 50 to 60 minutes, or until the juices run clear and the internal temperature of the thigh, when read on an instant-read meat thermometer, is 165°F. Grill: 375 °F Probe: 165 °F
6. Transfer the hens to a platter or plates and let rest for 5 minutes.
7. Garnish with a sprig of rosemary before serving. Enjoy!

Spatchcocked Turkey

Servings: 10-14

Cooking Time: 120 Minutes

Ingredients:

- 1 whole turkey
- 2 tablespoons olive oil
- 1 batch Chicken Rub

Directions:

1. Supply your smoker with wood pellets and follow the start-up procedure. Preheat the grill, with the lid closed, to 350°F.

2. To remove the turkey's backbone, place the turkey on a work surface, on its breast. Using kitchen shears, cut along one side of the turkey's backbone and then the other. Pull out the bone.

3. Once the backbone is removed, turn the turkey breast-side up and flatten it.

4. Coat the turkey with olive oil and season it on both sides with the rub. Using your hands, work the rub into the meat and skin.

5. Place the turkey directly on the grill grate, breast-side up, and cook until its internal temperature reaches 170°F.

6. Remove the turkey from the grill and let it rest for 10 minutes, before carving and serving.

Cider-brined Turkey

Servings: 8   Cooking Time: 180 Minutes

Ingredients:

- 1 whole turkey, about 12 to 14lb (4.5 to 5.4kg), thawed if frozen
- 1 white onion, peeled and sliced into quarters
- 1 apple, cut into wedges
- 2 celery stalks, sliced into 2-inch (5cm) pieces
- sprigs of fresh sage, rosemary, parsley, or thyme
- 8 tbsp unsalted butter, at room temperature
- coarse salt
- freshly ground black pepper
- for the brine
- 1 quart (1 liter) apple cider or apple juice
- 3 quarts (3 liters) cold distilled water
- ¾ cup coarse salt
- ½ cup light brown sugar or low-carb substitute
- 3 garlic cloves, peeled and smashed with a chef's knife
- 3 bay leaves

Directions:

1. In a large food-safe bucket, make the brine by combining the apple cider, water, salt, and brown sugar. Stir until the salt and sugar dissolve. Add the garlic and bay leaves. Submerge the turkey in the brine. If it floats, place a resealable bag of ice on top. Refrigerate for at least 8 hours and up to 16 hours.
2. Supply your smoker with wood pellets and follow the start-up procedure. Preheat the grill, with the lid closed, to 350° F.
3. Remove the turkey from the brine and pat dry with paper towels. Discard the brine. Place the onion, apple, celery, and herbs in the main cavity. Tie the legs together with butcher's twine. Fold the wings behind the back. Rub the outside with butter. Lightly season with salt and pepper.
4. Place the turkey breast side up on a wire rack in a shallow roasting pan. Place the pan on the grate and roast the turkey until the internal temperature in the thickest part of a thigh reaches 165°F (74°C), about 2½ to 3 hours.
5. Transfer the turkey to a cutting board and let rest for 20 minutes. (Save the drippings to make from-scratch turkey gravy.) Carve the turkey and arrange the meat on a large platter before serving.

Chicken Egg Rolls With Buffalo Sauce

Servings: 4   Cooking Time: 75 Minutes

Ingredients:

- 1/4 Cup Bleu Cheese, Crumbled
- 1/4 Cup Buffalo Sauce
- 1 Lb Chicken Breasts - Boneless, Skinless
- 4 Oz Cream Cheese, Softened
- 8 Egg Roll Wrappers
- 1/2 Jalapeno Pepper, Minced
- Pinch Sweet Heat Rub
- 1/4 Red Bell Pepper, Chopped
- 4 Scallion, Sliced Thin
- 1/4 Cup Sour Cream
- 2 Cups Vegetable Oil

Directions:

1. Supply your smoker with wood pellets and follow the start-up procedure. Preheat the grill, with the lid open, to 200° F. If using a gas or charcoal grill, set it up for low, indirect heat.
2. Season chicken breasts with Sweet Heat Rub, then place on the grill. Smoke for 1 hour, then remove from the grill, cool, shred, and set aside.
3. Prepare the filling: In a mixing bowl, use a hand mixer to blend cream cheese, bleu cheese, Buffalo sauce and sour cream.
4. Fold in scallions, jalapeño, red bell pepper, and shredded chicken.
5. Prepare egg rolls: Lay an egg roll wrapper on a flat surface and add 3 tablespoons of filling to the middle.
6. Fold the bottom of the wrapper over the top of the filling, then fold over each side. Brush the top point of the wrapper with warm water, then roll the wrapper tight. Transfer to a tray while filling the remaining wrappers.
7. Increase the temperature of the grill to 425°F, then set a cast iron Dutch oven on the grill. Add vegetable oil and heat for 5 minutes.
8. Place 3 egg rolls in heated oil and fry until golden, 1 to 2 minutes per side.
9. Transfer to a wire rack to cool, then fry the remaining egg rolls, in batches.
10. Cool egg rolls for 2 minutes, then slice in half and serve warm with celery sticks and extra Buffalo sauce for dipping.

VEGETABLES RECIPES

Roasted Pumpkin Seeds

Servings: 8

Cooking Time: 40 Minutes

Ingredients:
- 1 Whole Pumpkin, seeds
- olive oil or vegetable oil
- Jacobsen Salt Co. Pure Kosher Sea Salt

Directions:

1. As soon as possible after removing the seeds from the pumpkin, rinse pumpkin seeds under cold water in a colander and pick out the pulp and strings.
2. Place the pumpkin seeds in a single layer on an oiled baking sheet, stirring to coat. Supply your smoker with wood pellets and follow the start-up procedure. Preheat the grill, with the lid closed, to 180° F.
3. Place the baking sheet with the seeds on the grill grate, close the lid, and smoke for 20 minutes. Grill: 180 °F
4. Sprinkle your seeds with salt and turn the temperature on your grill up to 325°F. Roast the seeds until toasted, about 20 minutes. Check and stir seeds after the first 10 minutes. Grill: 325 °F
5. Seeds will be brown because they were smoked before being roasted. Enjoy!

Tater Tot Bake

Servings: 4

Cooking Time: 15 Minutes

Ingredients:

- 1 Whole frozen tater tots
- salt and pepper
- 1 Cup sour cream
- 1 Cup shredded cheddar cheese, divided
- 1/2 Cup bacon, chopped
- 1/4 Cup green onion, diced

Directions:

1. Supply your smoker with wood pellets and follow the start-up procedure. Preheat the grill, with the lid closed, to 375° F.
2. Line a baking sheet with aluminum foil for easy clean up and spread frozen tater tots onto sheet.
3. Sprinkle with Veggie Shake or salt and pepper to taste.
4. Place the baking sheet on the preheated grill grate and cook the tater tots for 10 minutes.
5. Drizzle sour cream over cooked tater tots.
6. Sprinkle the cheese, bacon bits and green onions on top of the tater tots.
7. Turn heat up to High heat and cook for 5 more minutes until the cheese melts and serve immediately. Enjoy!

Smoked Pickled Green Beans

Servings: 4

Cooking Time: 45 Minutes

Ingredients:

- 1 Pound Green Beans, blanched
- 1/2 Cup salt
- 1/2 Cup sugar
- 1 Tablespoon red pepper flakes
- 2 Cup white wine vinegar
- 2 Cup ice water

Directions:

1. Supply your smoker with wood pellets and follow the start-up procedure. Preheat the grill, with the lid closed, to 180° F.

2. Place the blanched green beans on a mesh grill mat and place mat directly on the grill grate. Smoke the green beans for 30-45 minutes until they've picked up the desired amount of smoke. Remove from grill and set aside until the brine is ready. Grill: 180 °F

3. In a medium sized saucepan, bring all remaining ingredients, except ice water, to a boil over medium high heat on the stove. Simmer for 5-10 minutes then remove from heat and steep 20 minutes more. Pour brine over ice water to cool.

4. Once brine has cooled, pour over the green beans and weigh them down with a few plates to ensure they are completely submerged. Let sit 24 hours before use. Enjoy!

Roasted Olives

Servings: 4

Cooking Time: 45 Minutes

Ingredients:

- 2 Cup mixed olives
- 3 Sprig fresh rosemary
- 2 Clove garlic, minced
- 2 Tablespoon orange zest
- 1/3 Cup extra-virgin olive oil
- 2 Tablespoon orange juice
- 1/2 Teaspoon red pepper flakes

Directions:

1. Combine the olives, rosemary, garlic, orange zest, red pepper flakes, olive oil, and orange juice in a glass oven-safe pie plate or baking dish. Cover with foil.

2. Supply your smoker with wood pellets and follow the start-up procedure. Preheat the grill, with the lid closed, to 300° F.

3. Roast the olives for 45 minutes, stirring once or twice. Serve warm in an attractive bowl. Enjoy! Grill: 300 °F

Roasted Jalapeno Cheddar Deviled Eggs

Servings: 6

Cooking Time: 30 Minutes

Ingredients:

- 7 Eggs, hard boiled
- 3 Tablespoon mayonnaise
- 1 Teaspoon brown mustard
- 1 Teaspoon apple cider vinegar
- 1 Dash hot sauce
- 1 jalapeño pepper, seeded and minced
- salt and pepper
- 1/2 Cup shredded cheddar cheese
- paprika

Directions:

1. Supply your smoker with wood pellets and follow the start-up procedure. Preheat the grill, with the lid closed, to 180° F.
2. Place your eggs directly on the grill grate and smoke for 30 minutes.
3. Remove from the grill and allow the eggs to cool. Smoking the eggs will give them a slightly yellowed color, but an intense smoky flavor. If a classic white egg is your preference, then skip this step.
4. Slice the eggs lengthwise and scoop the egg yolks directly into a gallon zip top bag.
5. Add the mayo, mustard, vinegar, hot sauce, roasted jalapeños and salt and pepper to the bag.
6. Zip the bag closed and, using your hands, knead all of the ingredients together in the bag until completely smooth.
7. Squeeze the yolk mixture into one corner of the bag and then cut the corner off. Pipe the yolk mixture into the whites.
8. Sprinkle with the finely shredded cheddar or paprika and chill until you are ready to serve. Enjoy!

Traeger Smoked Coleslaw

Servings: 8

Cooking Time: 20 Minutes

Ingredients:

- 1 Head purple cabbage, shredded
- 1 Head green cabbage, shredded
- 1 Cup shredded carrots
- 2 scallions, thinly sliced
- 1 1/2 Cup mayonnaise
- 1/8 Cup white wine vinegar
- 1 Teaspoon celery seed
- 1 Teaspoon sugar
- salt and pepper

Directions:

1. Supply your smoker with wood pellets and follow the start-up procedure. Preheat the grill, with the lid closed, to 180° F.
2. Spread cabbage and carrots out on a sheet tray and place directly on the grill grates. Smoke for 20 to 25 minutes or until cabbage picks up desired amount of smoke. Grill: 180 °F
3. Remove from grill and transfer to the refrigerator immediately to cool. While cabbage is cooling, make the dressing.
4. For the dressing, combine all ingredients in a small bowl and mix well.
5. Place smoked cabbage and carrots in a large bowl and pour dressing over them. Stir to coat well.
6. Transfer to a serving dish and sprinkle with scallions. Enjoy!

Baked Sweet Potato Casserole With Marshmallow Fluff

Servings: 6

Cooking Time: 60 Minutes

Ingredients:
- 3 Pound sweet potatoes
- 1/2 Cup milk
- 1 Cup brown sugar
- 3 eggs
- 4 Tablespoon butter
- 1/2 Teaspoon salt
- 3 egg white
- 1 Pinch salt
- 1 Pinch ground cinnamon

Directions:

1. Supply your smoker with wood pellets and follow the start-up procedure. Preheat the grill, with the lid closed, to 375° F.
2. Rinse, dry and pierce the sweet potatoes and place in grill whole. Cook for 45 minutes or until fork tender. Remove from grill and peel. Grill: 375 °F
3. Once peeled, mash the sweet potatoes in a large bowl with the milk, brown sugar, eggs, butter and salt. Place mashed potatoes in a baking dish and cook for 35 minutes. Grill: 375 °F
4. While the potatoes bake, make the fluff. Make a double boiler by bringing a small pot of water to a simmer, then placing the bowl of your stand mixer or another large stainless steel bowl atop the water.
5. Add the 3 egg whites, 2/3 cup brown sugar, a pinch of salt and a pinch of cinnamon to the bowl and whisk continuously until the sugar dissolves and the liquid is warm to the touch.
6. Transfer the bowl from the stovetop to your stand mixer and use the whisk attachment to whip the whites on medium-high speed until it turns glossy with stiff peaks, about 5-8 minutes.
7. Once the casserole has finished baking, use a rubber spatula to cover the sweet potato mixture with the fluff. Use the back of the spatula to create dramatic peaks.
8. Return to the grill for 5-7 minutes, or until the fluff starts to turn golden and the peaks are just shy of burnt. Remove from grill and enjoy!

Grilled Corn On The Cob With Parmesan And Garlic

Servings: 6

Cooking Time: 30 Minutes

Ingredients:

- 4 Tablespoon butter, melted
- 2 Clove garlic, minced
- salt and pepper
- 8 ears fresh corn
- 1/2 Cup shaved Parmesan
- 1 Tablespoon chopped parsley

Directions:

1. Supply your smoker with wood pellets and follow the start-up procedure. Preheat the grill, with the lid closed, to 450° F.
2. Place butter, garlic, salt and pepper in a medium bowl and mix well.
3. Peel back corn husks and remove the silk. Rub corn with half of the garlic butter mixture.
4. Close husks and place directly on the grill grate. Cook for 25 to 30 minutes, turning occasionally until corn is tender. Grill: 450 °F
5. Remove from grill, peel and discard husks. Place corn on serving tray, drizzle with remaining butter and top with Parmesan and parsley.

Red Potato Grilled Lollipops

Servings: 4

Cooking Time: 25 Minutes

Ingredients:
- 8 Large red bliss potatoes, halved
- 2 Clove garlic, minced
- 2 Sprig rosemary, minced
- 2 Tablespoon olive oil
- 1 Teaspoon salt
- 1/2 Teaspoon black pepper
- 5 Wooden Skewers, soaked in water
- 1/4 Cup Parmesan cheese, grated

Directions:
1. Supply your smoker with wood pellets and follow the start-up procedure. Preheat the grill, with the lid closed, to 450° F.
2. Halve potatoes and poke each several times with a fork.
3. Put the potatoes in a large bowl and toss with the minced garlic, rosemary leaves, a few tablespoons of olive oil, kosher salt, and pepper. Microwave the potatoes for 4 minutes. Gently toss potatoes and microwave for another 3 minutes.
4. Skewer potato halves threading about 4 or 5 potato halves on each skewer. Brush potatoes with olive oil.
5. Place the potato skewers on the Traeger, cut side down, and grill until the sides begin to brown (4-7 minutes).
6. Flip and grill skin side down for another 7-10 minutes.
7. They are done when a sharp knife tip easily penetrates the sides. Remove potatoes from grill and top with grated parmesan cheese. Enjoy!

Grilled Ratatouille Salad

Servings: 4

Cooking Time: 25 Minutes

Ingredients:

- 1 Whole sweet potatoes
- 1 Whole red onion, diced
- 1 Whole zucchini
- 1 Whole Squash
- 1 Large Tomato, diced
- vegetable oil
- salt and pepper

Directions:

1. Supply your smoker with wood pellets and follow the start-up procedure. Preheat the grill, with the lid closed, to High heat.
2. Slice all vegetables to a ¼ inch thickness.
3. Lightly brush each vegetable with oil and season with Traeger's Veggie Shake or salt and pepper.
4. Place sweet potato, onion, zucchini, and squash on grill grate and grill for 20 minutes or until tender, turn halfway through.
5. Add tomato slices to the grill during the last 5 minutes of cooking time.
6. For presentation, alternate vegetables while layering them vertically. Enjoy!

Smoked Jalapeño Poppers

Servings: 4

Cooking Time: 60 Minutes

Ingredients:
- 12 Medium jalapeño
- 6 Slices bacon, cut in half
- 8 Ounce cream cheese
- 2 Tablespoon Pork & Poultry Rub
- 1 Cup grated cheese

Directions:

1. Supply your smoker with wood pellets and follow the start-up procedure. Preheat the grill, with the lid closed, to 180° F. For optimal flavor, use Super Smoke if available.
2. Slice the jalapeños in half lengthwise. Scrape out any seeds and ribs with a small spoon or paring knife. Mix softened cream cheese with Traeger Pork & Poultry rub and grated cheese. Spoon mixture onto each jalapeño half. Wrap with bacon and secure with a toothpick.
3. Place the jalapeños on a rimmed baking sheet. Place on grill and smoke for 30 minutes. Grill: 180 °F
4. Increase the grill temperature to 375°F and cook an additional 30 minutes or until bacon is cooked to desired doneness. Serve warm, enjoy! Grill: 375 °F

Roasted Do-ahead Mashed Potatoes

Servings: 6

Cooking Time: 50 Minutes

Ingredients:

- 5 Pound Yukon Gold or russet potatoes
- 9 Tablespoon butter
- 8 Ounce cream cheese
- 1/2 Cup milk
- salt and pepper

Directions:

1. Peel the potatoes and cut into chunks that are roughly the same size. Cover with cold water and add a teaspoon of salt. Bring to a boil over high heat, then reduce the heat to medium and simmer the potatoes until they are tender.
2. Drain the potatoes and return them to the pot. Stir over low heat for 2 to 3 minutes to evaporate any excess moisture.
3. Mash the potatoes with a hand-held potato masher. (Alternative, rice the potatoes using a ricer.) Incorporate 8 tbsp butter and cream cheese. Add milk until the potatoes are of a good consistency. Stir in salt and pepper to taste.
4. Butter the inside of a casserole dish. Spread the potatoes out in an even layer in the casserole dish, smoothing the top with a spatula. Cool, cover, and refrigerate if not cooking right away. Before cooking, let the potatoes warm to room temperature (about an hour).
5. Supply your smoker with wood pellets and follow the start-up procedure. Preheat the grill, with the lid closed, to 350° F.
6. Bake the potatoes for 45 to 50 minutes, or until hot through. Grill: 350 °F

Roasted New Potatoes With Compound Butter

Servings: 4

Cooking Time: 45 Minutes

Ingredients:
- 2 Pound Small Red, White or Purple Potatoes (or Combination of All Three)
- 3 Tablespoon olive oil
- salt and pepper
- 2 Stick Butter, unsalted
- 1 Tablespoon shallot, minced
- 3 Tablespoon Finely Chopped Herbs, Such As Tarragon, Parsley, Basil or Combination
- 2 Teaspoon kosher salt

Directions:
1. Supply your smoker with wood pellets and follow the start-up procedure. Preheat the grill, with the lid closed, to 400° F. Cut the potatoes in half and place in a large mixing bowl. Cover with the olive oil, a teaspoon of salt and generous grinding of pepper.
2. Place on a large baking sheet so there is space between the potatoes. Place on the grill and roast for 45 minutes to 1 hour, until crispy skinned. Toss once during cooking. Grill: 400 °F
3. To make the butter: Place it in a medium sized shallow mixing bowl. Use a wooden spoon or strong spatula to break it up and soften it even more. Sprinkle the shallot, herbs, and salt over the butter, then use the spoon to combine the ingredients. Taste, adding more salt or herbs if necessary. Reserve a few tablespoons of the butter to serve on the potatoes.
4. To freeze the butter for future use, place a foot long piece of plastic wrap on the counter. Spread the butter out into a 6" log across the long direction of the plastic wrap towards the bottom. Begin to roll the plastic wrap away from you to roll it into a log, twisting the sides of the plastic wrap like a candy wrapper to secure.
5. Using your hands, shape the log into an even cylinder. Once it's wrapped tightly, place in the freezer. Then when more is needed, simply slice off coins of it to serve over grilled steak, chicken, veggies, or roasted potatoes. The butter holds well in the freezer for up to one month. Enjoy! *Cook times will vary depending on set and ambient temperatures.

Sicilian Stuffed Mushrooms

Servings: 6

Cooking Time: 25 Minutes

Ingredients:

- 12 Medium Fresh Mushrooms, about 1-1/2 inches in diameter
- 4 Ounce cream cheese, room temperature
- 1/4 Cup Parmesan cheese, grated
- 1/4 Cup shredded mozzarella cheese
- 8 Whole Pimento Stuffed Green Olives, chopped
- 3 Tablespoon Pepperoni, finely diced
- 1 1/2 Tablespoon Sun Dried Tomatoes, drained & minced
- 1/4 Teaspoon freshly ground black pepper

Directions:

1. Dampen a paper towel and wipe the outside of the mushrooms clean. Remove the stem. Using a small spoon, scoop out the inside of the mushroom leaving a shell.
2. Filling: In a small mixing bowl, beat together the cream cheese, Parmesan, and mozzarella. Stir in olives, pepperoni, tomatoes, basil, and pepper.
3. Mound the filling in the mushroom caps. Set each filled cap into the well of a muffin tin.
4. Supply your smoker with wood pellets and follow the start-up procedure. Preheat the grill, with the lid closed, to 350° F.
5. Arrange the muffin tin on the grill grate and bake the mushrooms for 25 to 30 minutes, or until the mushrooms are tender and the filling is beginning to brown.
6. Transfer to a serving plate or platter. Enjoy!

BEEF LAMB AND GAME RECIPES

Bbq Elk Shoulder

Servings: 4

Cooking Time: 240 Minutes

Ingredients:
- 6 Pound Elk, shoulder
- 12 Fluid Ounce beef broth
- 1 Whole meat injector
- 1 Tablespoon kosher salt
- 1 Tablespoon ground black pepper

Directions:
1. Take elk roast out of the fridge and allow to sit on counter for 30-60 minutes before cooking.
2. Supply your smoker with wood pellets and follow the start-up procedure. Preheat the grill, with the lid closed, to 225° F.
3. Inject the elk all over with beef broth. Combine salt and pepper and rub over entire roast.
4. Place on preheated grill and cook for 4 to 5 hours or until an instant read thermometer inserted in the thickest part of the meat registers 145°F. Remove from grill and allow to rest for 30 minutes before slicing. Grill: 225 °F Probe: 145 °F
5. Serve with baked beans, potato salad, coleslaw, white bread, Traeger BBQ sauce or your favorite BBQ sides and sauces. Enjoy!

Korean Style Bbq Prime Ribs

Servings: 5

Cooking Time: 480 Minutes

Ingredients:

- 3 lbs beef short ribs
- 2 tbsp sugar
- 3/4 cup water
- 1 tbsp ground black pepper
- 3 tbsp white vinegar
- 2 tbsp sesame oil
- 3 tbsp soy sauce
- 6 cloves garlic, minced
- 1/3 cup light brown sugar
- 1/2 yellow onion, finely chopped

Directions:

1. Combine soy sauce, water, and vinegar in a bowl. Mix and whisk in brown sugar, white sugar, pepper, sesame oil, garlic, and onion. Whisk until the sugars have completely dissolved

2. Pour marinade into large bowl or baking pan with high sides. Dunk the short ribs in the marinade, coating completely. Cover marinaded short ribs with plastic wrap and refrigerate for 6 to 12 hours3. Preheat pellet grill to 225°F.

3. Remove plastic wrap from ribs and pull ribs out of marinade. Shake off any excess marinade and dispose of the contents left in the bowl.

4. Place ribs on grill and cook for about 6-8 hours, until ribs reach an internal temperature of 203°F. Measure using a probe meat thermometer

5. Once ribs reach temperature, remove from grill and allow to rest for about 20 minutes. Slice, serve, and enjoy!

Rosemary Prime Rib

Servings: 8

Cooking Time: 60 Minutes

Ingredients:
- 1 (8 Lb) Prime Rib Roast
- 4 Tablespoon olive oil
- 4 Tablespoon tri-color peppercorns
- 3 Whole rosemary sprigs
- 3 Whole thyme sprigs
- 1/2 Cup garlic, minced
- 1/2 Cup Jacobsen Salt Co. Cherrywood Smoked Salt
- 4 Tablespoon Olive Oil

Directions:
1. Supply your smoker with wood pellets and follow the start-up procedure. Preheat the grill, with the lid closed, to 450° F.
2. Cut rib loin in half (roast halves separately for more controlled/even cooking.) Sear both halves in olive oil over very high heat until nice dark golden color.
3. Place tricolor peppercorns into a bag, crush pepper corns with a rolling pin.
4. Strip the leaves from the rosemary and thyme springs. Mix salt, crushed peppercorns, rosemary leaves, thyme leaves and garlic.
5. Pour olive oil over the rib loin and pour on the rub mix. Pat slightly to get it to stick to the meat.
6. Roast for 20-30 minutes on HIGH setting, then reduce heat to 300°F and roast for another 30 to 40 minutes or until a meat thermometer registers 125 degrees F for rare/medium rare (roast will continue to cook slightly after removing from the grill). Grill: 300 °F
7. Remove from the Traeger and let rest at least 20 minutes before slicing. Enjoy!

Bbq Bacon Meatballs

Servings: 4

Cooking Time: 60 Minutes

Ingredients:

- 1 Pound ground beef
- 1 egg
- 1/4 Cup milk
- 1/2 Cup breadcrumbs
- 2 Tablespoon Beef Rub
- 4 Strips bacon, cut in half
- 1/4 Cup Rub
- 1/2 Cup Apricot BBQ Sauce

Directions:

1. Mix beef, egg, milk, breadcrumbs and Traeger Beef Rub in a large bowl by hand. Once well mixed, make 2 ounce meatballs until complete.
2. Wrap each meatball with a half slice of bacon and slide toothpick all the way through.
3. Put Traeger Rub in a small bowl and roll each meatball in the rub until well coated.
4. Supply your smoker with wood pellets and follow the start-up procedure. Preheat the grill, with the lid closed, to 180° F.
5. Place the meatballs on the grate, close the lid and smoke for 1 hour. Grill: 180 °F
6. Increase the Traeger temperature to 350°F and preheat, lid closed for 15 minutes. Cook meatballs for another 20 to 30 minutes or until the internal temperature reaches 160°F to 165°F. Grill: 350 °F Probe: 160 °F
7. About 10 minutes before the meatballs are ready, brush with Traeger Apricot BBQ Sauce and allow it to caramelize.
8. Remove from grill and allow to rest for 5 minutes. Enjoy!

Smoked Pot Roast Brisket

Servings: 6

Cooking Time: 240 Minutes

Ingredients:

- 1 Coca-Cola, can
- 1 Heinz Chili Sauce, bottle
- 1 Dry Onion Soup Mix, package
- 4 Pound flat cut beef brisket

Directions:

1. Mix the Coke, Heinz chili sauce (you can find it in the condiment aisle of the grocery store) and dry onion soup mix in a bowl.
2. You'll want to trim the fat on the brisket, leaving only about 1/4 inch on top.
3. Put the brisket into a large baking pan and pour the Coke-chili sauce mixture over top. (If you use a larger piece of brisket, or the whole brisket you may need to double the sauce mixture.)
4. Supply your smoker with wood pellets and follow the start-up procedure. Preheat the grill, with the lid closed, to 300° F.
5. Put the pan of brisket on the grill and cook for 3 to 4 hours or until the brisket is tender. (Stick a fork in it and when it twists with little effort, it's ready!) Grill: 300 °F
6. Let the brisket rest, covered in its juices for 30 minutes to an hour before you slice her up and serve.

Smoked New York Steaks

Servings: 4

Cooking Time: 120 Minutes

Ingredients:

- 4 (1-inch-thick) New York steaks
- 2 tablespoons olive oil
- Salt
- Freshly ground black pepper

Directions:

1. Supply your smoker with wood pellets and follow the start-up procedure. Preheat the grill, with the lid closed, to 180°F.
2. Rub the steaks all over with olive oil and season both sides with salt and pepper.
3. Place the steaks directly on the grill grate and smoke for 1 hour.
4. Increase the grill's temperature to 375°F and continue to cook until the steaks' internal temperature reaches 145°F for medium-rare.
5. Remove the steaks and let them rest 5 minutes, before slicing and serving.

Roasted Mustard Crusted Prime Rib

Servings: 6

Cooking Time: 180 Minutes

Ingredients:

- 1 3-bone prime rib roast
- 1 Tablespoon black pepper
- 2 Tablespoon kosher salt
- 2 Tablespoon garlic, minced to a paste
- 1 Cup whole grain mustard

Directions:

1. Combine salt, black pepper, whole grain mustard and garlic in a small bowl and mix well. Rub mixture all over the exterior of the roast making sure each section is evenly coated.
2. Supply your smoker with wood pellets and follow the start-up procedure. Preheat the grill, with the lid closed, to 450° F.
3. Place the roast directly on the grill grate with the ribs facing the back of the grill. Close the lid and cook for 45 minutes or until the exterior of the roast has an even layer of browning. Grill: 450 °F
4. Reduce the temperature to 325 degrees F and continue to cook for 2.5 hours or until the internal temperature reaches 125 degrees F. Grill: 325 °F Probe: 125 °F
5. Remove roast from grill and allow to rest 15 minutes before slicing. After roast has rested, remove trussing and bones and slice into 1" inch sections. Enjoy!

Pan Seared Parsley Ribeye Steak

Servings: 2

Cooking Time: 20 Minutes

Ingredients:
- , 4 tbsp butter, room temp
- 1 tsp olive oil
- 1 tsp parsley, chopped
- tt chop house steak rub
- 1 ribeye steak, 1 to 1.5 inch thick
- 1 tsp scallion, sliced thin

Directions:

1. Season steak with Chop House Rub, then refrigerate for 1 hour.
2. In a small bowl, use a fork to mash up butter and 1 teaspoon of Chop House Rub. Transfer compound butter to a sheet of parchment paper, roll, and refrigerate for 1 hour.
3. Remove steak from the refrigerator, then place a covered cast iron skillet on the grill.
4. Supply your smoker with wood pellets and follow the start-up procedure. Preheat the grill, with the lid open, to 400° F.
5. If using a gas or charcoal grill, set it up for medium-high heat.
6. Remove the lid from the skillet. Open the sear slide. Add oil, then sear steak 1 to 2 minutes per side.
7. Add 3 tablespoons of butter ½ to 1 tablespoon at a time, tilting the pan, and using a spoon to baste the steak.
8. Continue searing, adding and basting with butter for an additional 3 to 5 minutes.
9. Remove steak from the skillet, rest for 5 minutes, then serve warm with additional compound butter and fresh herbs.

Savory Smoked Beef Short Ribs

Servings: 4

Cooking Time: 360 Minutes

Ingredients:
- 1 Cup Apple Cider Vinegar
- 1 Cup Apple Juice
- 4 Tablespoon Olive Oil
- 4 Tbsp Beef And Brisket Rub
- 2 1/2 Pounds (Or 6 Large) Beef Short Rib(S)

Directions:

1. Supply your smoker with wood pellets and follow the start-up procedure. Preheat the grill, with the lid closed, to 225° F.

2. In a food-safe spray bottle, combine the apple cider vinegar and apple juice. Set aside.

3. Flip the beef short ribs over, bone side up, and pull off the thick membrane. Discard. Flip the short ribs right side up and trim any excess fat from the top. Generously rub down the short ribs with olive oil and Beef and Brisket Rub.

4. Place the beef ribs on the center rack. Smoke for about 2 hours, until the short ribs have developed a crust and are a rich lacquered brown.

5. After 2 hours, remove the beef short ribs from the smoker, place in the heat-proof baking dish, and pour the apple cider vinegar and apple juice into the dish. Cover tightly with foil and smoke for another 1 ½-2 hours or until the ribs are fall-apart tender and register 200°F. Remove from the smoker and serve immediately.

Steak Tips With Mashed Potatoes

Servings: 4-6

Cooking Time: 60 Minutes

Ingredients:

- 1 Cup Beef Broth
- 1 Stick (Room Temperature) Butter, Unsalted
- 2 Tablespoon Flour, All-Purpose
- 1 Tablespoon Java Chophouse Seasoning
- 4 Tablespoon Java Chophouse Seasoning, Divided
- 2 Pounds Medium Russet Potatoes, Peeled And Cut (Large Chunks)
- 2 Pounds Strip Sirloin
- 1/2 To 1 Cup Whole Milk, Warm

Directions:

1. For the mashed potatoes: add the potatoes to a large pot and add enough cold water to cover the potatoes. Bring to a simmer over medium heat until the potatoes are tender enough to be pierced with a fork, about 40 minutes. Drain the potatoes.

2. Add the potatoes to a large mixing bowl. Add the butter, 1 tablespoon of Java Chop House and ½ cup of warm milk. Mash until smooth and lump free. If potatoes are too thick, add more milk, a tablespoon at a time, until you reach your desired consistency.

3. For the steak tips: Supply your smoker with wood pellets and follow the start-up procedure. Preheat the grill, with the lid closed, to 350° F. Season the steaks generously on both sides with 2 tablespoons of Java Chop House seasoning and grill for 8-10 minutes per side. When steaks are done, remove from grill, allow to rest for 15 minutes, then cut into chunks.

4. While the steak is resting, add the butter to a small saucepan over low heat. Once the butter is melted, whisk in the flour and cook for 2 minutes until the flour smells toasted. Slowly whisk in the beef broth and remaining 2 tablespoons of Java Chop House seasoning and cook the gravy over low heat until thickened. Remove from heat and toss the steak tips in the gravy.

5. Serve steak tips over mashed potatoes. Enjoy!

Texas Seared Beef

Servings: 4 Cooking Time: 150 Minutes

Ingredients:

- 1 cup beef stock
- 1/2 tsp black pepper
- 1/3 cup chili powder
- 1/2 tsp chipotle powder
- 2 1/2 lbs chuck roast, cut in 2-inch cubes
- to taste, cilantro
- 15 oz crushed tomatoes
- 1 tbsp cumin, ground
- 2 tbsp diced green chili peppers
- 3 garlic cloves, minced
- to taste, jalapeño
- 1 jalapeño, minced
- 1 1/2 tsp kosher salt
- 1 lime, zest & juice
- 1 tbsp olive oil
- 1 1/2 tsp oregano, dried
- to taste, red onion
- 1 red onion, diced
- to taste, sour cream

Directions:

1. Supply your smoker with wood pellets and follow the start-up procedure. Preheat the grill, with the lid closed, to 400° F. If using a gas or charcoal grill, set it up for medium-high heat. Set a deep cast iron skillet or Dutch oven on the grill and allow to preheat.
2. Place cubed chuck roast in a shallow pan then season with salt and pepper.
3. Add the oil to the Dutch oven then sear the beef on all sides. Remove seared beef and set aside.
4. Add the onions, garlic, and jalapeño to the pot. Stir then season with salt and pepper. Sauté for 3 minutes, then push all onions to the sides of the pot, creating a hole in the center. Add the chili powder, cumin, oregano, and green chilis. Cook for 1 minute, until the spices are fragrant, then reincorporate the onions. Stir in the beef stock, then bring to a hard simmer.
5. Return the seared beef to the Dutch oven, and stir to coat. Pour the crushed tomatoes in a single layer over the top of the beef. Cover the pot and reduce the grill temperature to 300 F. Braise the beef chili for 2 to 2 ½ hours, until beef is fork-tender.
6. Remove from the grill, then stir in lime zest and juice. Allow chili to sit for 10 minutes, then serve warm with your favorite chili toppings.

Grilled Garlic Tomahawk Steak

Servings: 1 - 2

Cooking Time: 60 Minutes

Ingredients:

- 3 Tablespoons Unsalted Butter
- 2 Tablespoons Chophouse Steak Seasoning
- 2 Garlic, Cloves
- Kosher Salt
- 1 Sprig Rosemary, Fresh
- 1, 2-Inch Thick Bone-In Tomahawk Ribeye

Directions:

1. Supply your smoker with wood pellets and follow the start-up procedure. Preheat the grill, with the lid closed, to 225° F.
2. Generously coat the tomahawk steak with kosher salt on all sides.
3. Allow the steak to sit at room temperature for one hour. After an hour, wipe off the salt and pat the steak dry.
4. Season the tomahawk steak with Chophouse Steak on both sides.
5. Place the steak on the grill grates, insert a temperature probe, and grill, undisturbed, for 45 minutes, or until the steak reaches an internal temperature of 120°F.
6. Remove the steak from the grill, tent with aluminum foil and allow it to rest for 10 minutes.
7. Place a cast iron skillet on the grill and increase the temperature of the to 450°F. Allow the pan to get as hot as possible.
8. Place the steak in the cast iron pan with the butter, garlic cloves, and rosemary sprig. Immediately begin spooning the butter over the steak as it melts.
9. Sear on one side for 1 minute.
10. Flip the steak, place the garlic and rosemary on top of the steak, and continue to baste the steak with the butter for another minute.
11. Pull the steak off the grill and allow it to rest for 10 minutes until the temperature rises to 130-135°F.
12. Pour the melted butter from the pan over the steak, slice, and serve immediately.

Savory Cheese Steak Rolls With Puff Pastry

Servings: 4   Cooking Time: 25 Minutes

Ingredients:

- 4 oz american or jack cheese, shredded, divided
- 2 tbsp butter
- to taste, chop house steak rub
- to taste, chop house steak rub (for sauce)
- 3 oz cream cheese
- 1 egg, beaten
- 1 tbsp flour
- 1 tbsp flour (for sauce)
- 1 puff pastry sheet, thawed
- 1 lb sandwich steak, shaved/sliced thin
- 1 tbsp vegetable oil
- 1 cup yellow onion, sliced thin
- 2/3 cup milk

Directions:

1. Supply your smoker with wood pellets and follow the start-up procedure. Preheat the grill, with the lid closed, to 400° F. If using a gas or charcoal grill, set it up for medium-high heat. Preheat the griddle to medium flame.

2. Add oil to the griddle, then cook steak for 2 to 3 minutes, turning with a spatula. Add onions, season with Chop House and cook another minute to soften. Transfer steak and onions to a bowl, then set aside to cool.

3. Meanwhile, melt butter in a sauté pan on the griddle. Stir in flour, then cook for 1 minute. Whisk in milk, then add cream cheese, and 2 ounces of shredded cheese. Whisk until smooth, then remove from the griddle to cool slightly. Use half of the sauce in the pastry, and the other half for serving/dipping once baked.

4. Flour your rolling surface, then set the pastry sheet on top of the flour. Roll the pastry sheet into a 10 to 12 inch square, then cut into 4 squares.

5. Spoon cheese sauce on each pastry square, then divide the steak and onion mixture among the pastries. Top each with remaining shredded cheese, brush sides with beaten egg, then fold pastries over, corner to corner. Secure the seams by pressing down with a fork. Brush the top with beaten egg, then place on a sheet tray.

6. Place the sheet tray on the grill and bake for 18 to 20 minutes, until golden. Remove from the grill, cool for 5 minutes, then cut in half and serve warm with cheese sauce.

Grilled Lemon Skirt Steak

Servings: 1-2

Cooking Time: 5 Minutes

Ingredients:

- 2 Cloves Garlic, Chopped
- 1 Lemon, Juice
- 2 Tablespoons Mustard, Grainy
- 1/4 Cup Olive Oil
- 2 Tablespoons Java Chophouse Seasoning
- 2 Pounds Skirt Steak, Trimmed
- 1 Tablespoon Worcestershire Sauce

Directions:

1. In a small bowl, mix together the Java Chophouse Seasoning, oil, garlic, lemon juice, and Worcestershire. Generously rub the mixture all over the skirt steak and allow to marinate for 45 minutes.
2. Supply your smoker with wood pellets and follow the start-up procedure. Preheat the grill, with the lid closed, to 400° F.
3. Grill the skirt steaks for 3-5 minutes on each side or until the steak is done to the desired degree of doneness.
4. Remove the steaks from the grill and allow to rest for 5 minutes before slicing and serving.

APPETIZERS AND SNACKS

Pigs In A Blanket

Servings: 4-6

Cooking Time: 15 Minutes

Ingredients:

- 2 Tablespoon Poppy Seeds
- 1 Tablespoon Dried Minced Onion
- 2 Teaspoon garlic, minced
- 2 Tablespoon Sesame Seeds
- 1 Teaspoon salt
- 8 Ounce Original Crescent Dough
- 1/4 Cup Dijon mustard
- 1 Large egg, beaten

Directions:

1. When ready to cook, start your smoker at 350 degrees F, and preheat with lid closed, 10 to 15 minutes.
2. Mix together poppy seeds, dried minced onion, dried minced garlic, salt and sesame seeds. Set aside.
3. Cut each triangle of crescent roll dough into thirds lengthwise, making 3 small strips from each roll.
4. Brush the dough strips lightly with Dijon mustard. Put the mini hot dogs on 1 end of the dough and roll up.
5. Arrange them, seam side down, on a greased baking pan. Brush with egg wash and sprinkle with seasoning mixture.
6. Bake in smoker until golden brown, about 12 to 15 minutes.
7. Serve with mustard or dipping sauce of your choice. Enjoy!

Chicken Wings With Teriyaki Glaze

Servings: 4

Cooking Time: 50 Minutes

Ingredients:

- 16 large chicken wings, about 3lb (1.4kg) total
- 1 to 1½ tbsp toasted sesame oil
- for the glaze
- ½ cup light soy sauce or tamari
- ¼ cup sake or sugar-free dark-colored soda
- ¼ cup light brown sugar or low-carb substitute
- 2 tbsp mirin or 1 tbsp honey
- 1 garlic clove, peeled, minced or grated
- 2 tsp minced fresh ginger
- 1 tsp cornstarch mixed with 1 tbsp distilled water (optional)
- for serving
- 1 tbsp toasted sesame seeds
- 2 scallions, trimmed, white and green parts sliced sharply diagonally

Directions:

1. Supply your smoker with wood pellets and follow the start-up procedure. Preheat the grill, with the lid closed, to 350° F.
2. Place the chicken wings in a large bowl, add the sesame oil, and turn the wings to coat thoroughly.
3. Place the wings on the grate at an angle to the bars. Grill for 20 minutes and then turn. Continue to cook until the wings are nicely browned and the meat is no longer pink at the bone, about 20 minutes more.
4. To make the glaze, in a saucepan on the stovetop over medium-high heat, combine the ingredients and bring the mixture to a boil. Reduce the glaze by 1/3, about 6 to 8 minutes. If you prefer your glaze to be glossy and thick, add the cornstarch and water mixture to the glaze and cook until it coats the back of a spoon, about 1 to 2 minutes more.
5. Transfer the wings to an aluminum foil roasting pan. Pour the glaze over them, turning to coat thoroughly. Place the pan on the grate and cook the wings until the glaze sets, about 5 to 10 minutes.
6. Transfer the wings to a platter. Scatter the sesame seeds and scallions over the top. Serve with plenty of napkins.

Bayou Wings With Cajun Rémoulade

Servings: 8　　　　　　　　　　　　Cooking Time: 40 Minutes

Ingredients:

- 16 large whole chicken wings or 32 drumettes and flats, about 3lb (1.4kg) total
- for the rub
- 1 tbsp kosher salt
- 1 tsp freshly ground black pepper
- 1 tsp paprika
- ½ tsp ground cayenne, plus more
- ½ tsp garlic powder
- ½ tsp celery salt
- ½ tsp dried thyme
- 2 tbsp vegetable oil
- for the rémoulade
- 1¼ cups reduced-fat mayo
- ¼ cup Creole-style or whole grain mustard
- 2 tbsp horseradish
- 2 tbsp pickle relish
- 1 tbsp freshly squeezed lemon juice
- 1 tsp paprika, plus more
- 1 tsp hot sauce, plus more
- 1 tsp Worcestershire sauce
- coarse salt
- for serving
- lemon wedges
- pickled okra (optional)

Directions:

1. Supply your smoker with wood pellets and follow the start-up procedure. Preheat the grill, with the lid closed, to 350° F.
2. If using whole wings, cut through the two joints, separating them into drumettes, flats, and wing tips. (Discard the wing tips or save them for chicken stock.) Alternatively, leave the wings whole. Place the chicken in a resealable plastic bag.
3. In a small bowl, make the rub by combining the ingredients. Mix well. Pour the rub over the wings and toss them to thoroughly coat. Refrigerate for 2 hours.
4. In a small bowl, make the Cajun rémoulade by whisking together the mayo, mustard, horseradish, pickle relish, lemon juice, paprika, hot sauce, and Worcestershire. Season with salt to taste. The mixture should be highly seasoned. Transfer to a serving bowl and lightly dust with paprika. Cover and refrigerate until ready to serve.
5. Remove the wings from the refrigerator and allow the excess marinade to drip off. Place the wings on the grate at an angle to the bars. Grill for 20 minutes and then turn. (They'll brown more evenly but will also have less of a tendency to stick.) Continue to cook until the wings are nicely browned and the meat is no longer pink at the bone, about 20 minutes more.
6. Remove the wings from the grill and pile them on a platter. Serve with the Cajun rémoulade, lemon wedges, and pickled okra (if using).

Cold-smoked Cheese

Servings: 6 Cooking Time: 180 Minutes

Ingredients:

- 2lb (1kg) well-chilled hard or semi-hard cheese, such as:
- Edam
- Gouda
- Cheddar
- Monterey Jack
- pepper Jack
- goat cheese
- fresh mozzarella
- Muenster
- aged Parmigiano-Reggiano
- Gruyère
- blue cheese

Directions:

1. Unwrap the cheese and remove any protective wax or coating. Cut into 4-ounce (110g) portions to increase the surface area.

2. If possible, move your smoker to a shady area. Place 1 resealable plastic bag filled with ice on top of the drip pan. This is especially important on a warm day because you want to keep the interior temperature of the grill between 70 and 90°F (21 and 32°C) or below.

3. Place a grill mat on one side of the grate. Place the cheese on the mat and allow space between each piece.

4. Fill your smoking tube or pellet maze (see Cast Iron Skillets and Grill Pans) with pellets or sawdust and light according to the manufacturer's instructions. Place the smoking tube on the grate near—but not on—the grill mat. When the tube is smoking consistently, close the grill lid.

5. Smoke the cheese for 1 to 3 hours, replacing the pellets or sawdust and ice if necessary. Monitor the temperature and make sure the cheese isn't beginning to melt. Carefully lift the mat with the cheese to a rimmed baking sheet and let the cheese cool completely before handling.

6. Package the smoked cheese in cheese storage paper or bags or vacuum-seal the cheese, labeling each. (While you can wrap the cheese tightly in plastic wrap, the cheese will spoil faster.) Let the cheese rest for at least 2 to 3 days before eating. It will be even better after 2 weeks.

Chorizo Queso Fundido

Servings: 4-6 Cooking Time: 20 Minutes

Ingredients:

- 1 poblano chile
- 1 cup chopped queso quesadilla or queso Oaxaca
- 1 cup shredded Monterey Jack cheese
- ¼ cup milk
- 1 tablespoon all-purpose flour
- 2 (4-ounce) links Mexican chorizo sausage, casings removed
- ⅓ cup beer
- 1 tablespoon unsalted butter
- 1 small red onion, chopped
- ½ cup whole kernel corn
- 2 serrano chiles or jalapeño peppers, stemmed, seeded, and coarsely chopped
- 1 tablespoon minced garlic
- 1 tablespoon freshly squeezed lime juice
- 1 teaspoon ground cumin
- 1 teaspoon salt
- 1 teaspoon freshly ground black pepper
- 1 tablespoon chopped fresh cilantro
- 1 tablespoon chopped scallions
- Tortilla chips, for serving

Directions:

1. Supply your smoker with wood pellets and follow the start-up procedure. Preheat, with the lid closed, to 350°F.
2. On the smoker or over medium-high heat on the stove top, place the poblano directly on the grate (or burner) to char for 1 to 2 minutes, turning as needed. Remove from heat and place in a closed-up lunch-size paper bag for 2 minutes to sweat and further loosen the skin.
3. Remove the skin and coarsely chop the poblano, removing the seeds; set aside.
4. In a bowl, combine the queso quesadilla, Monterey Jack, milk, and flour; set aside.
5. On the stove top, in a cast iron skillet over medium heat, cook and crumble the chorizo for about 2 minutes.
6. Transfer the cooked chorizo to a small, grill-safe pan and place over indirect heat on the smoker.
7. Place the cast iron skillet on the preheated grill grate. Pour in the beer and simmer for a few minutes, loosening and stirring in any remaining sausage bits from the pan.
8. Add the butter to the pan, then add the cheese mixture a little at a time, stirring constantly.
9. When the cheese is smooth, stir in the onion, corn, serrano chiles, garlic, lime juice, cuvmin, salt, and pepper. Stir in the reserved chopped charred poblano.
10. Close the lid and smoke for 15 to 20 minutes to infuse the queso with smoke flavor and further cook the vegetables.
11. When the cheese is bubbly, top with the chorizo mixture and garnish with the cilantro and scallions.
12. Serve the chorizo queso fundido hot with tortilla chips.

Delicious Deviled Crab Appetizer

Servings: 30

Cooking Time: 10 Minutes

Ingredients:

- Nonstick cooking spray, oil, or butter, for greasing
- 1 cup panko breadcrumbs, divided
- 1 cup canned corn, drained
- ½ cup chopped scallions, divided
- ½ red bell pepper, finely chopped
- 16 ounces jumbo lump crabmeat
- ¾ cup mayonnaise, divided
- 1 egg, beaten
- 1 teaspoon salt
- 1 teaspoon freshly ground black pepper
- 2 teaspoons cayenne pepper, divided
- Juice of 1 lemon

Directions:

1. Supply your smoker with wood pellets and follow the start-up procedure. Preheat, with the lid closed, to 425°F.
2. Spray three 12-cup mini muffin pans with cooking spray and divide ½ cup of the panko between 30 of the muffin cups, pressing into the bottoms and up the sides. (Work in batches, if necessary, depending on the number of pans you have.)
3. In a medium bowl, combine the corn, ¼ cup of scallions, the bell pepper, crabmeat, half of the mayonnaise, the egg, salt, pepper, and 1 teaspoon of cayenne pepper.
4. Gently fold in the remaining ½ cup of breadcrumbs and divide the mixture between the prepared mini muffin cups.
5. Place the pans on the grill grate, close the lid, and smoke for 10 minutes, or until golden brown.
6. In a small bowl, combine the lemon juice and the remaining mayonnaise, scallions, and cayenne pepper to make a sauce.
7. Brush the tops of the mini crab cakes with the sauce and serve hot.

Citrus-infused Marinated Olives

Servings: 6

Cooking Time: 30 Minutes

Ingredients:
- 1½ cups mixed brined olives, with pits
- ½ cup extra virgin olive oil
- 1 tbsp freshly squeezed lemon juice
- 1 garlic clove, peeled and thinly sliced
- 1 tsp smoked Spanish paprika
- 2 sprigs of fresh rosemary
- 2 sprigs of fresh thyme
- 2 bay leaves, fresh or dried
- 1 small dried red chili pepper, deseeded and flesh crumbled, or ¼ tsp crushed red pepper flakes
- 3 strips of orange zest
- 3 strips of lemon zest

Directions:

1. Supply your smoker with wood pellets and follow the start-up procedure. Preheat the grill, with the lid closed, to 180° F.
2. Drain the olives, reserving 1 tablespoon of brine. Spread the olives in a single layer in an aluminum foil roasting pan. Place the pan on the grate and cook the olives for 30 minutes, stirring the olives or shaking the pan once or twice.
3. In a small saucepan on the stovetop over low heat, warm the olive oil. Whisk in the lemon juice and the reserved 1 tablespoon of brine. Stir in the garlic and paprika. Add the rosemary, thyme, bay leaves, chili pepper, and orange and lemon zests. Warm over low heat for 10 minutes. Remove the saucepan from the heat.
4. Transfer the olives and olive oil mixture to a pint jar. Tuck the aromatics around the sides of the jar. Let cool and then cover and refrigerate for up to 5 days. Let the olives come to room temperature before serving.

Pulled Pork Loaded Nachos

Servings: 4   Cooking Time: 10 Minutes

Ingredients:

- 2 cups leftover smoked pulled pork
- 1 small sweet onion, diced
- 1 medium tomato, diced
- 1 jalapeño pepper, seeded and diced
- 1 garlic clove, minced
- 1 teaspoon salt
- 1 teaspoon freshly ground black pepper
- 1 bag tortilla chips
- 1 cup shredded Cheddar cheese
- ½ cup The Ultimate BBQ Sauce, divided
- ½ cup shredded jalapeño Monterey Jack cheese
- Juice of ½ lime
- 1 avocado, halved, pitted, and sliced
- 2 tablespoons sour cream
- 1 tablespoon chopped fresh cilantro

Directions:

1. Supply your smoker with wood pellets and follow the start-up procedure. Preheat, with the lid closed, to 375°F.
2. Heat the pulled pork in the microwave.
3. In a medium bowl, combine the onion, tomato, jalapeño, garlic, salt, and pepper, and set aside.
4. Arrange half of the tortilla chips in a large cast iron skillet. Spread half of the warmed pork on top and cover with the Cheddar cheese. Top with half of the onion-jalapeño mixture, then drizzle with ¼ cup of barbecue sauce.
5. Layer on the remaining tortilla chips, then the remaining pork and the Monterey Jack cheese. Top with the remaining onion-jalapeño mixture and drizzle with the remaining ¼ cup of barbecue sauce.
6. Place the skillet on the grill, close the lid, and smoke for about 10 minutes, or until the cheese is melted and bubbly. (Watch to make sure your chips don't burn!)
7. Squeeze the lime juice over the nachos, top with the avocado slices and sour cream, and garnish with the cilantro before serving hot.

Deviled Eggs With Smoked Paprika

Servings: 6   Cooking Time: 30 Minutes

Ingredients:

- 6 large eggs
- 3 tbsp reduced-fat mayo, plus more
- 1 tsp Dijon or yellow mustard
- ½ tsp Spanish smoked paprika or regular paprika, plus more
- dash of hot sauce
- coarse salt
- freshly ground black pepper
- for garnishing
- small sprigs of fresh parsley, dill, tarragon, or cilantro
- chopped chives
- minced scallions
- Mustard Caviar
- sliced green or black olives
- celery leaves
- sliced radishes
- diced bell peppers
- sliced cherry tomatoes
- fresh or pickled jalapeños
- sliced or diced pickles
- slivers of sun-dried tomatoes
- bacon crumbles
- smoked salmon
- Hawaiian black salt
- Caviar

Directions:

1. Supply your smoker with wood pellets and follow the start-up procedure. Preheat the grill, with the lid closed, to 180° F.

2. On the stovetop over medium-high heat, bring a saucepan of water to a boil. (Make sure there's enough water in the saucepan to cover the eggs by 1 inch [5cm].) Use a slotted spoon to gently lower the eggs into the water. Lower the heat to maintain a simmer. Set a timer for 13 minutes.

3. Prepare an ice bath by combining ice and cold water in a large bowl. Carefully transfer the eggs to the ice bath when the timer goes off.

4. When the eggs are cool enough to handle, gently tap them all over to crack the shell. Carefully peel the eggs. Rinse under cold running water to remove any clinging bits of shell, but don't dry the eggs. (A damp surface will help the smoke adhere to the egg whites.)

5. Place the eggs on the grate and smoke until the eggs take on a light brown patina from the smoke, about 25 minutes. Transfer the eggs to a cutting board, handling them as little as possible.

6. Slice each egg in half lengthwise with a sharp knife. Wipe any yolk off the blade before slicing the next egg. Gently remove the yolks and place them in a food processor. Pulse to break up the yolks. Add the mayo, mustard, paprika, and hot sauce. Season with salt and pepper to taste. Pulse until the filling is

smooth. Add additional mayo 1 teaspoon at a time if the mixture is a little dry. (It shouldn't be too loose either.)

7. Spoon the filling into each egg half or pipe it in using a small resealable plastic bag. You can also use a pastry bag fitted with a fluted tip.

8. Place the eggs on a platter and lightly dust with paprika. Accompany with one or more of the suggested garnishes.

Pig Pops (sweet-hot Bacon On A Stick)

Servings: 24
Cooking Time: 30 Minutes

Ingredients:
- Nonstick cooking spray, oil, or butter, for greasing
- 2 pounds thick-cut bacon (24 slices)
- 24 metal skewers
- 1 cup packed light brown sugar
- 2 to 3 teaspoons cayenne pepper
- ½ cup maple syrup, divided

Directions:
1. Supply your smoker with wood pellets and follow the start-up procedure. Preheat, with the lid closed, to 350°F.
2. Coat a disposable aluminum foil baking sheet with cooking spray, oil, or butter.
3. Thread each bacon slice onto a metal skewer and place on the prepared baking sheet.
4. In a medium bowl, stir together the brown sugar and cayenne.
5. Baste the top sides of the bacon with ¼ cup of maple syrup.
6. Sprinkle half of the brown sugar mixture over the bacon.
7. Place the baking sheet on the grill, close the lid, and smoke for 15 to 30 minutes.
8. Using tongs, flip the bacon skewers. Baste with the remaining ¼ cup of maple syrup and top with the remaining brown sugar mixture.
9. Continue smoking with the lid closed for 10 to 15 minutes, or until crispy. You can eyeball the bacon and smoke to your desired doneness, but the actual ideal internal temperature for bacon is 155°F
10. Using tongs, carefully remove the bacon skewers from the grill. Let cool completely before handling.

Jalapeño Poppers With Chipotle Sour Cream

Servings: 8   Cooking Time: 45 Minutes

Ingredients:

- 3 strips of thin-sliced bacon
- 12 large jalapeños, red, green, or a mix
- 8oz (225g) light cream cheese, at room temperature
- 1 cup shredded pepper Jack, Monterey Jack, or Cheddar cheese
- 1 tsp chili powder
- ½ tsp garlic salt
- smoked paprika
- for the sour cream
- 1¼ cups light sour cream
- juice of ½ lime
- ½ to 1 canned chipotle peppers in adobo sauce, finely minced, plus 1 tsp of sauce, plus more
- 1 tbsp minced fresh cilantro leaves
- ½ tsp coarse salt, plus more

Directions:

1. Supply your smoker with wood pellets and follow the start-up procedure. Preheat the grill, with the lid closed, to 375° F.
2. Line a rimmed sheet pan with aluminum foil and place a wire rack on top. Place the bacon in a single layer on the wire rack. Place the pan on the grate and grill until the bacon is crisp and golden brown, about 20 minutes. Transfer the bacon to paper towels to cool and then crumble. Set aside.
3. In a small bowl, make the chipotle sour cream by whisking together the ingredients. Add more salt, chipotle peppers, or adobe sauce to taste. Cover and refrigerate.
4. Slice the jalapeños lengthwise through their stems. Scrape out the veins and seeds with the edge of a small metal spoon.
5. In a small bowl, beat together the cream cheese, shredded cheese, chili powder, and garlic salt. Stir in the crumbled bacon. Mound the cream cheese mixture in the jalapeño halves. Line another rimmed sheet pan with aluminum foil and place a wire rack on top. Place the jalapeños filled side up in a single layer on the wire rack.
6. Place the sheet pan on the grate and roast the jalapeños until the filling has melted and the peppers have softened, about 20 to 25 minutes. (They should no longer look bright in color.) Remove the pan from the grill and let the peppers rest for 5 minutes.
7. Transfer the poppers to a platter and lightly dust with paprika. Serve with the chipotle sour cream.

Grilled Guacamole

Servings: 6

Cooking Time: 30 Minutes

Ingredients:

- 3 large avocados, halved and pitted
- 1 lime, halved
- ½ jalapeño, deseeded and deveined
- ½ small white or red onion, peeled
- 2 garlic cloves, peeled and skewered on a toothpick
- 1 tsp coarse salt, plus more
- 1½ tbsp reduced-fat mayo
- 2 tbsp chopped fresh cilantro
- 2 tbsp crumbled queso fresco (optional)
- tortilla chips

Directions:

1. Supply your smoker with wood pellets and follow the start-up procedure. Preheat the grill, with the lid closed, to 225° F.

2. Place the avocados, lime, jalapeño, and onion cut sides down on the grate. Use the toothpicks to balance the garlic cloves between the bars. Smoke for 30 minutes. (You want the vegetables to retain most of their rawness.)

3. Transfer everything to a cutting board. Remove the garlic cloves from the toothpick and roughly chop. Sprinkle with the salt and continue to mince the garlic until it begins to form a paste. Scrape the garlic and salt into a large bowl.

4. Scoop the avocado flesh from the peels into the bowl. Squeeze the juice of ½ lime over the avocado. Mash the avocados but leave them somewhat chunky. Finely dice the jalapeño. Dice 2 tablespoons of onion. (Reserve the remaining onion for another use.) Add the jalapeño, onion, mayo, and cilantro to the bowl. Stir gently to combine. Taste for seasoning, adding more salt, lime juice, and jalapeño as desired.

5. Transfer the guacamole to a serving bowl. Top with the queso fresco (if using). Serve with tortilla chips.

Sriracha & Maple Cashews

Servings: 10

Cooking Time: 60 Minutes

Ingredients:

- 2 tbsp unsalted butter
- 3 tbsp pure maple syrup
- 1 tbsp sriracha
- 1 tsp coarse salt (use only if nuts are unsalted)
- 2½ cups unsalted cashews

Directions:

1. Supply your smoker with wood pellets and follow the start-up procedure. Preheat the grill, with the lid closed, to 250° F.
2. In a small saucepan on the stovetop over low heat, melt the butter. Add the maple syrup, sriracha, and salt (if using). Stir until combined. Add the nuts and stir gently to coat thoroughly.
3. Spread the nuts in a single layer in an aluminum foil roasting pan coated with cooking spray. Place the pan on the grate and smoke the nuts until they're lightly toasted, about 1 hour, stirring once or twice.
4. Remove the pan from the grill and let the nuts cool for 15 minutes. They'll be sticky at first but will crisp up. Break them up with your fingers and store at room temperature in an airtight container, such as a lidded glass jar.

Bacon-wrapped Jalapeño Poppers

Servings: 12

Cooking Time: 30 Minutes

Ingredients:

- 8 ounces cream cheese, softened
- ½ cup shredded Cheddar cheese
- ¼ cup chopped scallions
- 1 teaspoon chipotle chile powder or regular chili powder
- 1 teaspoon garlic powder
- 1 teaspoon salt
- 18 large jalapeño peppers, stemmed, seeded, and halved lengthwise
- 1 pound bacon (precooked works well)

Directions:

1. Supply your smoker with wood pellets and follow the start-up procedure. Preheat, with the lid closed, to 350°F. Line a baking sheet with aluminum foil.
2. In a small bowl, combine the cream cheese, Cheddar cheese, scallions, chipotle powder, garlic powder, and salt.
3. Stuff the jalapeño halves with the cheese mixture.
4. Cut the bacon into pieces big enough to wrap around the stuffed pepper halves.
5. Wrap the bacon around the peppers and place on the prepared baking sheet.
6. Put the baking sheet on the grill grate, close the lid, and smoke the peppers for 30 minutes, or until the cheese is melted and the bacon is cooked through and crisp.
7. Let the jalapeño poppers cool for 3 to 5 minutes. Serve warm.

COCKTAILS RECIPES

Smoked Mulled Wine

Servings: 10

Cooking Time: 60 Minutes

Ingredients:

- 2 Bottle red wine
- 1/2 Cup whiskey
- 1/2 Cup white rum
- 1/2 Cup honey
- 1 cinnamon stick
- 2 pods star anise
- 4 whole cloves
- 1 (3 in) orange peel

Directions:

1. Supply your smoker with wood pellets and follow the start-up procedure. Preheat the grill, with the lid closed, to 180° F.
2. In a shallow baking dish, combine wine, whiskey, rum, honey, cinnamon stick, star anise, cloves and orange peel. Stir well until combined.
3. Place the dish directly on the grill grate and smoke for one hour until the mixture is warm. Grill: 180 °F
4. Remove from grill and ladle into mugs leaving the mulling spices behind. Garnish with fresh cinnamon sticks, anise, orange zest or a combination. Enjoy!

Bacon Old-fashioned Cocktail

Servings: 2

Cooking Time: 20 Minutes

Ingredients:

- 16 Slices bacon
- 1/2 Cup warm water (110°F to 115°F)
- 1500 mL bourbon
- 1/2 Fluid Ounce maple syrup
- 4 Dash Angostura bitters
- 2 fresh orange peel

Directions:

1. Smoke bacon prior to making Old Fashioned using this recipe for Applewood Smoked Bacon.
2. To Make Bacon: Supply your smoker with wood pellets and follow the start-up procedure. Preheat the grill, with the lid closed, to 325° F.
3. Place bacon in a single layer on a cooling rack that fits inside a baking sheet pan. Cook in Traeger for 15-20 minutes or until bacon is browned and crispy. Reserve bacon for later. Let the fat cool slightly; you'll use the fat to infuse the bourbon. Grill: 325 °F
4. Combine 1/4 cup of warm (not hot) liquid bacon fat with the entire contents of a 750ml bottle of bourbon in a glass or heavy plastic container.
5. Use a fork to stir well. Let it sit on the counter for a few hours, stirring every so often.
6. After about four hours, put bourbon fat mixture into the freezer. After about an hour, the fat will congeal and you can simply scoop it out with a spoon. You can fine-strain the mixture through a sieve to remove all fat if desired.
7. Combine ingredients with ice and stir until cold. Strain over fresh ice in an Old Fashioned glass and garnish with reserved bacon and orange peel. Enjoy!

Traeger Old Fashioned

Servings: 2

Cooking Time: 60 Minutes

Ingredients:

- 2 orange
- 2 Cup cherries
- 3 Ounce bourbon
- 1 Ounce Smoked Simple Syrup
- 8 Dash Bitters Lab Apricot Vanilla Bitters

Directions:

1. Supply your smoker with wood pellets and follow the start-up procedure. Preheat the grill, with the lid closed, to 180° F.
2. While Traeger preheats, slice whole orange into wheels.
3. Place cherries on a small sheet pan and place in the Traeger. Place orange slices directly on the grill grate.
4. Smoke cherries for 1 hour and oranges for 25 minutes, depending on taste, before removing from the grill. Let oranges and cherries cool. Grill: 180 °F
5. Pour bourbon into glass, followed by Traeger Smoked Simple Syrup and bitters. Add ice and stir for 45 seconds or until drink is well-diluted.
6. Strain contents into new glass over fresh ice. Skewer orange wheel and add cherry for garnish. Enjoy!

Smoked Apple Cider

Servings: 2

Cooking Time: 30 Minutes

Ingredients:
- 32 Ounce apple cider
- 2 cinnamon sticks
- 4 whole cloves
- 3 star anise
- 2 Pieces orange peel
- 2 Pieces lemon peel

Directions:

1. Supply your smoker with wood pellets and follow the start-up procedure. Preheat the grill, with the lid closed, to 225° F.
2. Combine the cider, cinnamon stick, star anise, clove, lemon and orange peel in a shallow baking dish.
3. Place directly on the grill grate and smoke for 30 minutes. Remove from grill, strain and transfer to four mugs. Grill: 225 °F
4. Finish with a slice of apple and a cinnamon stick to serve. Enjoy!

Grilled Peach Sour Cocktail

Servings: 2

Cooking Time: 15 Minutes

Ingredients:

- 2 peach, sliced
- 2 Tablespoon sugar
- 1 1/2 Ounce Smoked Simple Syrup
- 4 Ounce bourbon
- 6 Dash Bitters Lab Apricot Vanilla Bitters
- 2 Sprig fresh thyme, for garnish

Directions:

1. Supply your smoker with wood pellets and follow the start-up procedure. Preheat the grill, with the lid closed, to 325° F.
2. Toss peach slices with granulated sugar and place directly on grill grate. Cook for 20 minutes or until grill marks form. Remove from grill and let cool. Grill: 325 °F
3. Place peaches and Traeger Smoked Simple Syrup into tin and muddle. Peaches should form about an ounce of juice during the muddling. Once completed, add remaining ingredients and shake.
4. Pour contents into glass over fresh ice and garnish with fresh thyme. Enjoy!

Traeger Gin & Tonic

Servings: 2

Cooking Time: 45 Minutes

Ingredients:
- 1/2 Cup berries
- 2 orange, sliced
- 4 Tablespoon granulated sugar
- 3 Ounce gin
- 1 Cup tonic water
- 2 Sprig fresh mint, for garnish

Directions:

1. Supply your smoker with wood pellets and follow the start-up procedure. Preheat the grill, with the lid closed, to 180° F.

2. For the Smoked Berries: Spread mixed fresh berries on a sheet pan and place directly on the grill grate. Smoke for 30 minutes then remove from grill. Grill: 180 °F

3. For the Orange Slices: Increase the grill temperature to 450°F and preheat, lid closed for 15 minutes. Grill: 450 °F

4. Toss the orange slices with granulated sugar and place directly on grill grate. Cook for about 5 minutes, turning once or until the slices have developed grill marks. Grill: 450 °F

5. Pour gin into a glass, add ice and berries, then top with tonic water. Garnish with a fresh mint sprig and grilled orange wheel. Enjoy!

Smoked Eggnog

Servings: 4

Cooking Time: 60 Minutes

Ingredients:

- 2 Cup whole milk
- 1 Cup heavy cream
- 4 egg yolk
- Cup sugar
- 3 Ounce bourbon
- 1 Teaspoon vanilla extract
- 1 Teaspoon nutmeg
- 4 egg white
- whipped cream

Directions:

1. Plan ahead, this recipe requires chill time.
2. Supply your smoker with wood pellets and follow the start-up procedure. Preheat the grill, with the lid closed, to 180° F.
3. Pour the milk and the cream into a baking pan and smoke on the Traeger for 60 minutes. Grill: 180 °F
4. Meanwhile, in the bowl of a stand mixer, beat the egg yolks until they lighten in color. Gradually add 1/3 cup sugar and continue to beat until sugar completely dissolves.
5. After the milk and cream have smoked, add them along with the bourbon, vanilla and nutmeg into the egg mixture and stir to combine.
6. Place the egg whites in the bowl of a stand mixer and beat to soft peaks. When you lift the beaters the whites will make a peak that slightly curls down.
7. With the mixer still running, gradually add 1 tablespoon of sugar and beat until stiff peaks form.
8. Gently fold the egg whites into the cream mixture and then whisk to thoroughly combine.
9. Chill eggnog for a couple hours to let the flavors meld. Garnish with a dash of nutmeg and whipped cream on top. Enjoy!

Smoked Berry Cocktail

Servings: 2

Cooking Time: 15 Minutes

Ingredients:

- 1/2 Cup strawberries, stemmed
- 1/2 Cup blackberries
- 1/2 Cup blueberries
- 8 Ounce bourbon or iced tea
- 2 Ounce lime juice
- 3 Ounce simple syrup
- soda water
- fresh mint, for garnish

Directions:

1. Supply your smoker with wood pellets and follow the start-up procedure. Preheat the grill, with the lid closed, to 180° F.
2. Wash berries well, spread them on a clean cookie sheet and place on the grill. Smoke berries for 15 minutes. Grill: 180 °F
3. Remove berries from grill and transfer to a blender. Puree berries until smooth then pass through a fine mesh strainer to remove seeds.
4. To create a layered cocktail, pour 2 ounces of berry puree in the bottom of a glass. Next, pour 2 ounces of bourbon or iced tea over the back of a spoon into the glass, then 1/2 ounce lime juice and 1/2 ounce simple syrup, top with soda water and ice. Finish with mint or extra berries for garnish.
5. Repeat the same process for 3 more servings. Enjoy!

In Traeger Fashion Cocktail

Servings: 2
Cooking Time: 20 Minutes

Ingredients:

- 2 Whole orange peel
- 2 Whole lemon peel
- 3 Ounce bourbon
- 1 Ounce Smoked Simple Syrup
- 6 Dash Bitters Lab Charred Cedar & Currant Bitters

Directions:

1. Supply your smoker with wood pellets and follow the start-up procedure. Preheat the grill, with the lid closed, to 350° F.
2. Place the lemon and orange peel directly on the grill grate and cook 20 to 25 minutes or until lightly browned. Grill: 350 °F
3. Add bourbon, Traeger Smoked Simple Syrup and bitters to a mixing glass and stir over ice. Stir until glass is chilled and contents are well diluted.
4. Strain into a new glass over fresh ice and garnish with grilled lemon and orange peel. Enjoy!

Smoked Raspberry Bubbler Cocktail

Servings: 2

Cooking Time: 45 Minutes

Ingredients:
- 2 Cup fresh raspberries
- Smoked Simple Syrup
- 8 Ounce sparkling wine

Directions:

1. Supply your smoker with wood pellets and follow the start-up procedure. Preheat the grill, with the lid closed, to 180° F.

2. Smoked Raspberry Syrup: Place 1 cup fresh raspberries on a grill mat and smoke for 30 minutes. Grill: 180 °F

3. After the raspberries have been smoked, set a few aside for garnish. Place the remainder into a shallow sheet pan with Traeger Smoked Simple Syrup. Place back on the grill grate and let smoke for 45 minutes. Remove from heat and allow to cool. Strain and refrigerate until ready to use. Grill: 180 °F

4. Place 1 ounce of the smoked raspberry syrup in the bottom of a champagne flute and top off with sparkling white wine or champagne.

5. Garnish with smoked raspberries. Enjoy!

Smoked Hibiscus Sparkler

Servings: 4

Cooking Time: 30 Minutes

Ingredients:

- 1/2 Cup sugar
- 2 Tablespoon dried hibiscus flowers
- 1 Bottle sparkling wine
- crystallized ginger, for garnish

Directions:

1. Supply your smoker with wood pellets and follow the start-up procedure. Preheat the grill, with the lid closed, to 180° F.
2. Place water in a shallow baking dish and place directly on the grill grate. Smoke the water for 30 minutes or until desired smoke flavor is achieved. Grill: 180 °F
3. Pour water into a small saucepan and add sugar and hibiscus flowers. Bring to a simmer over medium heat and cook until sugar is dissolved.
4. Strain out the hibiscus flowers and transfer your simple syrup to a small container and refrigerate until chilled.
5. Pour 1/2 ounce smoked hibiscus simple syrup in the bottom of a champagne glass and top with sparkling wine.
6. Drop in a few pieces of crystallized ginger to garnish. Enjoy!

Cran-apple Tequila Punch With Smoked Oranges

Servings: 2

Cooking Time: 15 Minutes

Ingredients:

- 6 Cup apple juice, chilled
- 6 Cup light cranberry cocktail
- 1 Cup cranberries, fresh or thawed
- 3 Large oranges, halved
- 1 Cup sugar, for rimming glasses
- 2 Tablespoon lemon juice
- 2 Cup reposado tequila
- 1 Cup orange-flavored liqueur, such as Grand Marnier or Cointreau
- 2 Bottle sparkling wine (such as prosecco) or sparkling water

Directions:

1. Combine 1 cup each of the apple and cranberry juices, then pour into ice cube trays. If the cube molds are big enough, place a few cranberries into each cube. Freeze for 6 hours to overnight.

2. Supply your smoker with wood pellets and follow the start-up procedure. Preheat the grill, with the lid closed, to 180° F.

3. Place the orange halves cut-side down on the grill and smoke for 15 minutes. Remove from the grill and juice oranges. Reserve smoked orange juice. Grill: 180 °F

4. When ready to serve, place the sugar on a flat plate. Pour the lemon juice into a bowl that will fit the rim of each glass.

5. Carefully dip the rim of each glass in the lemon juice, then dip in the sugar to create a 1/8" sugar rim. Turn the glass right-side up and allow to dry for a few minutes before using.

6. Just before serving, mix the remaining apple juice, cranberry cocktail and smoked orange juice with the tequila, orange liqueur, and sparkling wine in a large bowl or pitcher. Taste, adding more of any ingredient to meet your preference.

7. When ready to serve, place a few ice cubes in each glass, then pour a cup of the punch over the top. Alternatively, place all of the ice cubes in the punch bowl and allow guests to help themselves. Enjoy!

www.ingramcontent.com/pod-product-compliance
Lightning Source LLC
Chambersburg PA
CBHW081417080526
44589CB00016B/2565